MANIFEST THAT SHIT

Real Stories. Real Manifestations

Written by:

Karyn Medeiros

MANIFEST THAT SHIT

Copyright © 2025 by Karyn Medeiros All rights reserved. No part of this publication may be reproduced, distributed, or transmitted in any form or by any means, including photocopying, recording, or other electronic or mechanical methods, without the prior written permission of the publisher, except in the case of brief quotations embodied in critical reviews and certain other noncommercial uses permitted by copyright law.

Any use of information in this book is at the reader's discretion and risk. Neither the publisher nor author can be held responsible for any loss, claim, or damage arising out of the use or misuse of the suggestions made.

MANIFEST THAT SHIT

FOREWARD

Welcome to the world of manifestation, where the empowering teachings of Karyn Medeiros, along with her certified manifestation students and coaches, come together to share their transformative journeys in Manifest That Shit!

As one of Karyn's early mentors and friends, I am beyond thrilled to witness not only her evolution but also the incredible growth of her dedicated students and coaches. Together, they offer unique perspectives and rich experiences that highlight the true power of manifesting your reality.

In this collective masterpiece of real-life manifestations, you'll embark on a journey guided by Karyn's expertise and the authentic stories of those she's inspired. Each testimony serves as a beacon of inspiration, revealing the diverse paths and profound transformations that manifestation can bring into your life.

Karyn's approach is grounded in authenticity, and her gift for simplifying the complexities of manifestation shines through in every chapter. With practical advice, personal anecdotes, and deep insights, this book is more than a manifesting manual—it's a heartfelt invitation to embrace your true potential and create the life you desire.

Through the shared wisdom and genuine experiences in these pages, you'll uncover the tools, mindset shifts, and unwavering belief needed to manifest like a badass. Karyn and her collaborators present a holistic approach that celebrates self-discovery, resilience, and the innate power within us all.

Prepare to be uplifted, inspired, and motivated as you dive into this book—a powerful resource of knowledge and empowerment. Let Karyn and her team be your guides on this transformational journey, and get ready to manifest that shit!

With boundless anticipation,

Christina Whiteley

Business Mentor & Friend

CEO of Life Transformed

MANIFEST THAT SHIT

INTRODUCTION

I wanted to fill this book with as many manifestation stories as possible. I've been blessed beyond belief through manifestation (though trust me, life wasn't always sunshine and rainbows), and now I feel this pull to share what I've learned—along with the experiences of others. I want you to know that you can change your life in an instant.

Yeah, I know. That probably sounds like total bullshit. But honestly, I can't explain it any other way. Life is magical. Once you learn a few key principles, you can shift your reality into something you've only dreamed of—and faster than you'd believe.

Think of this book as the manifestation version of Chicken Soup for the Soul. You know, those heartwarming stories that make you think, Wow, if they can do it, maybe I can too! I want this to be a collection of inspiring, life-changing stories that fill you with that same hope and belief in yourself.

Keep this book close. When doubt creeps in, I want you to pick up this bad boy and remind yourself what's possible.

Here's how I made it happen:

I personally reached out to some of my students who've experienced jaw-dropping transformations through manifestation. (And yes, I'm being dramatic on purpose—because some of these stories are fucking jaw-dropping.) I asked them to share their best stories here to inspire you.

My hope? As you read, you'll start to perk up and think, Okay, let's give this a shot. I'm ready to change my life. I want to manifest an incredible life just like they did.

So, what can you expect?

You're about to dive into a book packed with incredible, transformative, true-life manifestation stories from women I'm proud to call my friends. And as you read, I want you to pause and ask yourself: Could this happen to me?

Spoiler alert: The answer is YES. If these women (and yours truly) can do it, so can you. All you need is a little spark of belief. So grab that belief—even if it's just a tiny flicker right now—and hold on tight as we jump into stories that just might change your life.

Let's go.

MANIFEST THAT SHIT

TABLE OF CONTENTS

FOREWARD	v
INTRODUCTION	viii
CHAPTER 1	**2**
The Universe Heard Me.. 2	
CHAPTER 2	**7**
Husband: Manifested.. 7	
CHAPTER 3	**11**
The 4 Year Promise To Motherhood.. 11	
CHAPTER 4	**17**
Manifesting the Million-Dollar Dream Home........................ 17	
CHAPTER 5	**23**
Manifesting an iPad in Three Weeks..23	
CHAPTER 6	**28**
Bingo, Slots, and a Florida Family Vacation..........................28	
CHAPTER 7	**32**
The Universe Wrote This Chapter..32	
CHAPTER 8	**36**
Manifested 30 pounds - Gonzo..36	
CHAPTER 9	**42**
My Viral Manifestation Method.. 42	
CHAPTER 10	**52**
THE DAY WE MET SANTA CLAUS... 52	

CHAPTER 11 — 61

THE REFLECTION IN THE MIRROR: FINDING MYSELF THROUGH GRIEF, HEALING, LOVE AND MANIFESTATION..................61

CHAPTER 12 — 71

STARS, SIGNS, AND SECOND CHANCES.................. 71

CHAPTER 13 — 88

AWAKENING POTENTIAL: A WOMAN'S JOURNEY OF RESILIENCE, EMPOWERMENT AND MANIFESTATION............................ 88

CHAPTER 14 — 102

EMBRACING THE MAGIC OF TRUST.................. 102

CHAPTER 15 — 116

THE POWER WITHIN: FOLLOWING THE NUDGES THROUGH EXPANSION & RESILIENCE TO FIND CONFIDENCE AND FULFILLMENT.... 116

CHAPTER 16 — 142

THE JOURNEY IS THE DESTINATION: A SINGLE MUM'S STORY OF PERSEVERANCE AND TRIUMPH......................... 142

CHAPTER 17 — 161

GRATITUDE IN THE STORM: THE KEY TO UNLOCKING MIRACLES..... 161

CHAPTER 18 — 174

FAITHFUL MANIFESTATION: ALIGNING WITH GOD'S PLAN FOR AN ABUNDANT LIFE......................... 174

CHAPTER 19 — 185

MANIFESTING A NEW ME: REDEFINING MY PURPOSE AND POWER 185

CHAPTER 20 — 201

AGAINST ALL ODDS: A MANIFESTATION STORY OF STRENGTH, FAITH, AND SUCCESS..201

CHAPTER 21   **212**

FROM HOT MESS TO HEALING: HOW MY DARKEST DAYS LED TO MY GREATEST TRANSFORMATION.. 212

ACKNOWLEDGMENTS   **234**

> Manifestation is like ordering at a restaurant. You put in your order, trust it's being made, and stop asking the chef when it'll be ready.

@KARYNMEDEIROS

CHAPTER 1

The Universe Heard Me

First, I want you to understand something important: we are manifesting every single day. Our thoughts constantly shape our reality—whether they're good or bad. It doesn't matter; both manifest.

I've chosen some personal stories to share with you. Some are big, life-changing transformations, and others are smaller but just as powerful. I want to show you that no matter how big or small your desires are, they all have the potential to manifest.

Let's start with one of my earliest manifestations.

As a little girl, I remember sitting in the back seat of my parents' car, driving down the highway. I'd stare out the window at these huge skyscrapers and think, I want to work in one of those buildings someday. I had no idea why. Maybe it was the shiny glass or how tall and impressive they looked, but in my mind, anyone who worked there had to be successful.

Every time we drove by, I'd daydream about working in one of those buildings. I didn't know what kind of work people did inside them—hell, I didn't care. I just knew I wanted to be there.

Around that same time, I also started saying I wanted to own my own business someday. (Most of my uncles, grandfathers, and my dad were all self-employed.) Again, I had no clue what kind of business it would be, but I kept repeating that desire to myself.

I was probably eight or nine years old when I began planting those seeds, and those dreams stuck with me through the years.

Fast forward to adulthood. My first job was as a restaurant hostess, which led to many years of waitressing while I went to college, paid my rent, and struggled to stay afloat. I moved out on my own at 20 and spent the next decade scraping by. Honestly, I struggled for much longer—probably 10 to 15 years—but let's just focus on those early 10 years for now.

By the time I was 28 or 29, I was offered a corporate job in Toronto… in one of the tallest buildings downtown. The moment I walked in, I was hit with this overwhelming realization: Holy shit, I made it! I'm successful. I'm working in one of those glass buildings I dreamed about as a kid.

It felt amazing… for a while. And then reality hit. Corporate life sucked. The politics, the stress, the endless bullshit—I hated it. But I kept working in those tall glass buildings for the next 10 years, give or take.

Here's the thing about manifestation: the Universe will always give you what you ask for—or something better. I had focused on that image of working in a skyscraper for so long that the Universe delivered exactly that. But over time, I realized it wasn't aligned with my highest good. I still wanted to own my own business, but I just didn't know what that business looked like.

Then one day, the Universe threw me an opportunity that changed everything. I was in corporate, miserable, unhealthy from all the stress, and begging the Universe for something better—something that would make me happy and bring in more money. Despite having decent-paying jobs, both my husband and I were still living paycheck to paycheck.

One night, I was scrolling through Facebook when I saw a post about this magical mascara. I bought it, loved it, and learned I could make money selling it. Long story short, I joined and started selling mascara while still working as a corporate manager, overseeing a team of underwriters who decided whether people got approved for mortgages.

Fast forward a year, and that magical mascara income replaced my corporate income. In January 2015, I became a full-time business owner.

Now, I don't sell mascara anymore, but that manifestation was a pivotal moment. It completely shifted the trajectory of my life. I finally experienced the freedom I had dreamed about as a little girl—freedom of time, money, and opportunities.

This transformation happened because I was open to receiving it. The Universe didn't just hand me the perfect plan. It challenged me with an opportunity that didn't look like I expected, but it turned out to be exactly what I needed. (Read that again!)

And that's how manifestation works. You don't get to decide how things will unfold. The Universe handles that part. Your job is to stay open to receive, even when the path doesn't look like what you had in mind.

Sometimes, manifestations take years to come through. This one took many years, but I believe I had to go through those struggles to be ready for what I have today. Over a decade ago, I finally understood the power of manifestation. That's when my journey really began. And it's been magic ever since.

CHAPTER 2

Husband: Manifested

The next pivotal part of my manifestation journey was manifesting my husband. Yes, you read that right—I manifested my husband.

As a teenager (or maybe even younger, who knows?), I started dreaming about the kind of guy I wanted to marry. And since I've been a to-do list junkie for as long as I can remember, of course, I wrote it all down. Seriously, I live and breathe lists. I make multiple to-do lists every day to keep me on track and help me crush my goals. Clearly, this trait started early!

I remember telling my friends exactly what I wanted in my future husband and jotting down all the details. Here are some of the things I absolutely remember writing on that list:

- European
- Dark hair
- Nice tan
- Nice ass
- Big lips
- Good father
- Treats me well

Shares responsibilities 50/50

Fast forward to today. Here's my husband:

- He's European, born in Portugal, and moved to Canada at 13.
- He's got a natural tan, dark hair, and, yes, big, juicy lips. Oh, and a great ass too.
- He's an incredible, hands-on dad, he loves me, and always puts our family first.
- I literally married the man I had visualized and dreamed about for years.

But here's the real point of this story: You are always manifesting—whether you realize it or not. Whatever you consistently focus on, you will attract into your life. If you're stuck in negative thinking, that's exactly what you'll manifest—more struggle, more negativity, more things you don't want. But if you shift your focus to positive thoughts, desires, and goals, you'll start attracting good things.

It's not about knowing when your manifestation will appear. You can't always control the timing. But if you carry an unwavering belief that it will come, chances are it'll arrive sooner than you expect.

I didn't perform some elaborate manifestation ritual to meet my husband. I simply got crystal clear on what I wanted and held that vision in my mind. Over time, the Universe guided me through some pretty dark challenges and detours, preparing me for the relationship I was destined for.

And yes, I went through plenty of BS before meeting him. If you've read my first book, you know I hit a lot of dead ends with deadbeat men. But I never lost the belief that my dream hubby was out there. And eventually, the Universe came through, just like it always does when you stay aligned with your desires.

> The Universe doesn't respond to begging. It responds to belief.

@KARYNMEDEIROS

CHAPTER 3

The 4-Year Promise To Motherhood

The next pivotal manifestation in my journey was my first son, Mateo. Yes, I manifested my children too.

Joe and I struggled with infertility for years. After we got married, we decided to start building our family, but nothing happened. We tried and tried, but still no pregnancy. Eventually, we saw a doctor and learned we'd need fertility treatment because, according to medical science, my eggs were "older." I got married at 33—not exactly old—but apparently, in egg years, I was pushing it.

By the time I was 34, then 35, we still hadn't conceived. The fertility clinic became like a second home to us.

Anyone who's experienced infertility knows how emotionally and physically draining the process is. Month after month, I'd go in for blood work, only to get the same devastating call later that day: "You're not pregnant." The disappointment was brutal. I did get pregnant once with the help of fertility drugs, but it was an ectopic pregnancy that had to be terminated before it became life-threatening.

After a few years of this, I reached my breaking point. My body and spirit couldn't take it anymore. The stress was overwhelming. It was taking a toll on our marriage, which was still relatively new. We were barely holding it together. So, we made a pact. We agreed to stop trying for children and leave it in the hands of the Universe. If it was meant to be, it would happen. If not, we'd accept it.

We decided to get a dog instead. We talked about how we'd spoil the hell out of this dog, treat it like our baby, and make it a full part of our family. A couple of months later, we found Max—a yellow lab (though he's more orange than yellow). We picked him out in May and brought him home on July 5.

We loved this guy (and 12 years later, we still do!)

And wouldn't you know it... by the end of August, after months of fertility treatments and completely letting go of the pressure, I found out I was pregnant.

Here's what I realized later: there were two crucial shifts that helped this manifestation come through.

- **We surrendered**. We let go of the need to control how and when the manifestation would happen. We stopped obsessing and trusted that if it was meant to be, it would come.
- **We shifted focus.** By turning our attention to loving and caring for Max instead of stressing about having a baby, we created space for the Universe to do its thing.

But wait, it gets better.

As a teenager or young adult (I can't remember exactly), I used to tell my friends that I wanted to be married for four years before having kids. I believed a strong bond was crucial to surviving the challenges of parenthood—sleepless nights, financial stress, and the general chaos that comes with a new baby. And for some reason, I thought four was the perfect gap.

Well, guess what day our first child was born?

Mateo was born on our fourth wedding anniversary.

Four years later, TO THE EXACT DAY.

Yes, you heard that right.

The Universe delivered my manifestation down to the exact date.

At the time, I didn't even remember that I had said I wanted to wait four years. It wasn't until everything unfolded that I thought, Holy shit, I manifested this entire situation. But now that I've learned so much about manifestation, I also understand that you need to be very specific with your desires.

I had focused on being married for four years before having kids, but I wasn't specific about how that timeline would play out. Because of that, I had to go through four years of challenges to get there. The Universe will always give you what you want, but sometimes it has to rearrange things in ways you don't expect.

That's a key lesson in manifesting: Be clear, be intentional, and don't leave the details up to chance unless you're okay with a wild ride.

Once Mateo was born, I also manifested exactly what I'd always wanted with my second son, Tiago.

As a kid, I used to say I wanted my children to be two years apart, just like my sisters and me. Sure enough, 25 months after Mateo, Tiago was born.

These manifestations all stemmed from desires I planted as a child. I didn't know the manifestation principles I teach today, but the seeds were still there. Now, knowing what I know, I realize how important it is to teach our children to focus on what they want and to be specific. When you do that, you can help them avoid unnecessary challenges on their path to achieving their dreams.

My son Mateo, who is 10 at the moment, knows and tells me all the time, "My brain doesn't know what is real or fake; it only knows what I tell it." I've been telling him this for years.

Focus on what you want (NOT WHAT YOU DON'T WANT), and everything will manifest right to you.

That is one powerful gift you can give your kids now too.

The Universe always delivers. But clarity and trust are your greatest allies.

> You can't manifest a dream life with a shitty mindset. Fix your thoughts, and the rest will follow.

@KARYNMEDEIROS

CHAPTER 4

Manifesting the Million-Dollar Dream Home

Let me tell you how I manifested the house I'm living in now—a million-dollar home I didn't think I had any business manifesting at the time.

By this point, I'd dabbled in manifestation enough to know it worked, even if I wasn't 100% sure how it worked. Joe and I were living in our cozy 1,100-square-foot townhouse. It was our first home, and it served us well, but the kids were growing fast.

Mateo was 3 ½, Tiago was 1 ½, and with school just around the corner, I wanted to move to a neighbourhood near a good school. You know what I mean, right?

The only problem? We didn't exactly have the funds to make a big move. We made good money, but we were still living paycheck to paycheck. However, life was starting to shift. I was running my mascara business full-time, and things were picking up financially. Joe and I decided it was time to look for a detached home we could grow into for years to come.

We knew the area we wanted—and we also knew it was expensive. But I was determined. At the time, I was learning more about vision boards and how to manifest through visualization. I made a vision board filled with images of the dream home I wanted:

- A white, open-concept kitchen
- White marble floors
- A stunning curved staircase
- A spacious, green backyard with no neighbours behind us

I even told our realtor, "If the kitchen isn't white, don't even show me the listing." I was that serious about my vision!

So, we started looking at houses. We made offers on five or six properties over a few months, but every single one was declined. No matter how much over the asking price we offered, someone else always swooped in with better conditions.

Looking back now, I'm grateful those offers didn't work out. Honestly, a few of those houses were just desperation bids—I can't imagine living in them now.

At that point, I knew enough about manifestation to realize these houses weren't fully aligned with my vision. None of them had everything I wanted. I was willing to settle, but deep down, I knew I shouldn't.

So, we decided to pause the search and take a break for six months.

A month or so later, while lying in bed, I came across a new listing. It wasn't in our target area—it was 30 minutes away—but something about it caught my attention. I texted our realtor and asked him to book an appointment for Monday.

When we arrived, I knew this was it. The house was gorgeous. The second I walked through the door, I saw white marble floors and a stunning curved staircase, just like the pictures on my vision board. The open-concept design was exactly what I had envisioned, and the kitchen was all white (well, except for some weird green walls and a black backsplash, but that was an easy fix).

We stepped outside, and the backyard was spacious, backing onto a ravine with no neighbours behind us—just nature. It was perfect. I turned to Joe and said, "Okay, this is the one."

We put in an offer, and after some negotiation, the owners accepted. But then we hit a roadblock. The house appraised $30,000 less than the purchase price. I wasn't willing to pay the difference out of pocket, and the sellers refused to lower the price. Just like that, the deal fell through.

I was devastated. I had already started packing, knowing that taking aligned action was part of the manifestation process. But the Universe had other plans.

After a couple of days of feeling crushed, I surrendered. I told the Universe, If this house is truly meant for us, you'll make it happen. And if not, I trust that you'll lead us to something even better.

Three weeks later, our realtor called. The sellers had changed their minds and agreed to reduce the price. We signed the deal and moved in 30 days later.

Now, here's the lesson in all of this:

Manifestations don't always unfold the way you expect. I thought we'd be living in a different neighbourhood, in a house that checked most of my boxes. But the Universe had something better in store—something that aligned with my vision down to the smallest details.

When things don't work out, I want you to remember this: the Universe may be rerouting you to something greater. It may not happen as quickly as it did for us, but if you can have faith, surrender, and let go of the need to control how your manifestation unfolds, you'll be amazed at what shows up.

Trust the process. The Universe always delivers.

> You're not broke. You're temporarily financially rearranging for bigger blessings.

@KARYNMEDEIROS

CHAPTER 5

Manifesting an iPad in Three Weeks

Let me tell you about the time I manifested a brand-new iPad—and fast! This manifestation came through in just three weeks, and it taught me a lot about the power of clear intention and surrender.

Here's how it all went down.

One night, I was lying in bed, frustrated because my iPad kept glitching. I turned to my husband and said, "I want a new iPad because this one's driving me crazy." He casually replied, "Okay, then just go get one."

But I wasn't feeling it. "No," I said. "I don't want to pay for it. I want to manifest it somehow because I'm not spending $700 on a new iPad."

And that was it. I didn't sit down and visualize, make a vision board, or repeat affirmations. I just stated exactly what I wanted with strong energy and intention—and then... I forgot about it.

Now, before you think manifestation is always that simple, let me explain. It doesn't always work by just thinking about something once and having it magically show up. But in this case, I believe it happened quickly because my intention was so clear when I said those words to my husband. My energy was laser-focused at that moment. Once I put the intention out there, I let go completely. I didn't obsess over how it would happen or when. I simply trusted that it would come.

At the time, I was transitioning into my business. I was still involved with my network marketing company but was moving to a new one. I had no clue how quickly that shift would unfold, but within a week, I joined a new company and hit the ground running.

Here's the wild part. Shortly after, I found out that the company was offering a bonus. If you reached a certain rank or sales goal, you could choose a free reward: an iPad, an Apple Watch, $300 cash, or a shopping voucher.

I had already hit the bonus without even knowing those prizes were an option! I wasn't working toward the iPad specifically—I didn't even know it was on the table. But when they told me I'd earned a reward, I immediately knew what to choose. Of course, I picked the iPad.

And just like that, three weeks after casually telling my husband I wanted a new iPad without paying for it, I had exactly what I'd asked for.

Manifestation Lesson

This experience taught me two important things about manifestation:

1. **Clear Intention Matters:** When I said I wanted a new iPad, my intention was crystal clear, and the energy behind it was strong. I wasn't wishy-washy. I knew what I wanted.
2. **Surrendering Works:** After I stated my intention, I didn't worry about how or when it would happen. I trusted the Universe to handle the details and went on with my life. That surrender created space for the manifestation to come through naturally and quickly.

Sometimes, manifestations require more effort and time, but other times, when you're aligned with strong focus and energy, things can come together almost effortlessly. This was one of those times.

Remember: the key is to set your intention clearly, trust that the Universe will deliver, and then let go of the need to control the process.

And when it shows up, it might just blow your mind—just like my iPad manifestation did.

Stop putting 'Plan B' energy into your 'Plan A' dreams.

@KARYNMEDEIROS

CHAPTER 6

Bingo, Slots, and a Florida Family Vacation

A couple of years ago, the kids really wanted to go to Florida. So, we decided that would be our family vacation for the year. But here's the thing—I didn't want to pay for the trip out of our checking account. Why? Because I knew I could manifest the money instead.

This wasn't like my iPad manifestation, where I just stated what I wanted and let it go. This time, I had to take aligned action and get really clear with the Universe about what I wanted.

To manifest the money for our trip, I needed to plan everything as though I already had the funds. I had to step into the energy of someone who was booking a real vacation.

Here's what that looked like:

- I planned where we would stay and calculated the cost of the hotel or resort.
- I looked up flights and estimated the cost of airline tickets, including when we'd fly and how much it would be for the time of year we wanted to go.
- I budgeted for a rental car, figuring out what kind of car we'd need and how long we'd need it.
- I estimated our spending money, including groceries, snacks, and meals.
- I added a budget for shopping and entertainment.

After pulling it all together, I had my number: $4,000. That's how much we'd need for the trip.

These aligned actions were my signal to the Universe that this trip was happening. I didn't just say, "Hey Universe, I want $4,000." I put energy and intention behind it through planning. Once I got clear on the amount, I simply asked the Universe out loud to send me $4,000 to pay for the trip.

Then I let it go.

I didn't write anything down. I didn't stress over how it would come to me. I didn't set a deadline, though I did say, "as soon as possible." I surrendered the outcome and trusted that the Universe would handle the rest.

Around the third or fourth week after making my request, I went to bingo with a friend. Yes, I love bingo. I don't go often—LOL—but it's always a blast. This particular bingo hall also had casino slots, and let me tell you, those machines were always packed. People would come just for the slots or play them during intermission.

Now, I'd never played the slots at intermission before. I usually just hung out and chatted until the next bingo game started. But that night, something nudged me. My friend asked, "Are you going to play the slots?" and I thought, You know what? I think I am.

I pulled out $60 and walked over to the Wheel of Fortune dollar machine. I put in the money and started playing. After spending around $30 or so, THE JACKPOT WENT OFF.

Want to guess how much the jackpot was?

You got it: exactly $4,000.

A few weeks later, off to Florida, we went.

> Start acting like the badass you're manifesting.

@KARYNMEDEIROS

CHAPTER 7

The Universe Wrote This Chapter

For many years, I had this dream of writing my own book. I didn't know what I'd write about exactly, but the desire was always there, like a quiet whisper telling me, One day, you'll do this. I figured that eventually, a topic would reveal itself and something I was passionate about and could teach others.

A little over a decade ago, I started a manifestation and gratitude-based business with one of my best friends. We were both dabbling in manifestation, and things were starting to take off for us. We ran that business together for about two years, but unfortunately, the partnership didn't work out the way we'd hoped.

Now, don't get me wrong, we're still friends, and I love her. But when you're in a 50-50 business partnership, things can get tricky, especially when your goals and visions begin to diverge on different paths.

During that time, I often thought about writing a book on manifestation, maybe even creating a playbook to help people learn how to manifest. But I didn't want to co-author it. I knew deep down that I wanted to write it myself. However, since we owned the business together, I figured that dream would have to stay on hold.

When the partnership ended, it was tough. It took me a while to come to terms with it, but I knew it was the right move. Sometimes, relationships or opportunities need to shift to make space for something new.

After I went solo and started building my own Manifestation and Mindset Education business, I finally realized that this was my time. Within the first year of running my new business, I decided that I was going to write that book. And when I say it was a last-minute decision, I mean it. I gave myself about three months to finish it before the end of the year.

I buckled down, wrote the book, published it, and the rest is history. That book became a massive success and still sells hundreds of copies every month. I'm endlessly grateful for how it all played out, and I have no doubt this book will follow the same path.

The manifestation lesson in this is sometimes, things need to fall apart to make room for your manifestations. For me, it meant letting go of a business partnership that I cherished. While I missed the daily connection of working with my best friend, I trusted that this shift was necessary for something better to come into my life.

And that's exactly what happened.

When the Universe takes something away, it's not to punish you, it's to prepare you for what's next. It may hurt at the moment, but if you hold onto the belief that something better is on its way, you'll be amazed at what unfolds.

For me, that "something better" was the opportunity to step into my true purpose and make a bigger impact with my vision for all of you.

Trust the process.

When one door closes, the Universe is already working on opening the next one.

MANIFEST THAT SHIT

> Gratitude is the cheat code to manifesting faster.

@KARYNMEDEIROS

CHAPTER 8

Manifested 30 pounds - Gonzo

I don't know if you can relate to this, but I've been on a weight-loss rollercoaster for the last 10 years.

Before having kids, I was always really thin. There was only one year where I gained a lot of weight, but as soon as I broke up with that boyfriend, the weight magically disappeared (funny how that works, right?). Other than that, I never had to think about my weight until I became a mum.

When I got pregnant with my first son, I gained 75 pounds. Honestly, it mostly was all my fault. I was in the best shape of my life before the pregnancy, going to the gym six days a week, and I thought I could crush Big Macs without a care in the world because I'd just lose the weight right after. Spoiler alert: that's not how it went.

I had a C-section and didn't recover as quickly as I thought I would. I couldn't get back to the gym until six months postpartum. And if you've had kids, you know how those early months go with zero sleep, survival mode, eating whatever's convenient just to stay sane.

By the time I finally started getting it together, I found out I was pregnant with my second son. Since I hadn't fully lost the weight from my first pregnancy, I was already starting this one at a higher weight. I tried to stay healthier the second time around, but I still gained more weight.

The Yo-Yo Diet Years

For years after that, I tried every diet under the sun, starving myself, choking down cabbage soup, and drinking lemon water with cayenne pepper. You name it, I probably tried it. Every diet would last about a week before I'd go back to my old habits.

It wasn't until I fully understood the power of manifestation and the mind that things started to change. I asked myself, Can I manifest weight loss? And with that, I decided to approach it differently. I wouldn't just focus on actions like dieting or exercising. I was going to shift my mindset and step into the version of myself who had already lost weight.

Becoming "Her"

To manifest my weight loss, I had to embody the version of myself that was already 30 pounds lighter. I made a list of things that this future version of me would do differently and then started playing the part.

1. **Dress the Part**

    I had been living in oversized sweatshirts and leggings every day. I told myself, If I were 30 pounds lighter, I'd dress in cute clothes. So, I bought two cute outfits that I loved and made a point to wear them regularly. Did I feel amazing in them? Nope. But I kept going because I knew this was how "she" would dress. I had to step into that version of myself.

2. **Tuck It In**

    This one was tough. After two C-sections and too much sugar, I had a belly I was not proud of. I always wore untucked shirts to hide it. But I knew that if I were my future self, I'd be tucking my shirts in confidently. So, I started tucking them in even though it made me super uncomfortable. I was stepping into her energy, belly and all.

3. **Move My Body**

   I asked myself, How would she move her body? I didn't think I'd want to work out every day, but I knew I'd want to walk regularly for both physical and mental health. So, I made a 100-day challenge for myself to walk every single day. I'm now on my third 100-day challenge and have walked almost 300 days in a row. If I missed a day, I had to restart from day one, which kept me motivated not to screw up.

4. **Show Love to My Body**

   Every day, while brushing my teeth, I'd look in the mirror and say, "I love you," ten times. I knew that if I didn't show my body love, it would never change in the way I wanted. When I walked past mirrors, I'd pretend I liked what I saw and say, "Looking good, Karyn!" Even if I didn't believe it at first, I kept acting as if.

5. **Eat Like Her**

   I asked myself, Would the future me be eating this junk right now? The answer was always no. That gave me the motivation to stop eating crap. I didn't go on a strict diet, but I started eating in a way that aligned with the healthier version of myself.

The Transformation

After stepping into this new mindset and lifestyle, the weight literally started falling off. I lost 30 pounds I had struggled to lose for years (like years!) Once I got clear on what I wanted and embodied the version of myself who had already achieved it, everything clicked.

If you're struggling with weight loss (or any other goal), I highly encourage you to try this approach. Think about your future self, the version of you who has already achieved your goal. What would they do? How would they dress, move, and eat? Write down those steps and start embodying them today.

This isn't about perfection. It's about shifting your mindset and aligning your actions with the energy of who you want to become.

Take a before and after photo. Challenge yourself. And watch what happens when you step into the version of yourself that already exists in your dreams.

> If you keep focusing on what's missing, that's exactly what you'll keep getting—more of nothing.

@KARYNMEDEIROS

CHAPTER 9

My Viral Manifestation Method

Alright, I'm leaving you with one last manifestation story. Honestly, I could've filled this entire book with my own stories, but I wanted to share a variety of stories from other incredible manifestos so you wouldn't just be stuck with mine. But I couldn't end without sharing this one, because it was a game-changer for me.

This is the story of how I manifested $41,900 in just 30 days—and it all started with a challenge.

At the time, my business coach challenged me to manifest $20,000 in 30 days. The kicker? She wanted me to write down every single step I took during the process so I could eventually share those steps with others. I accepted the challenge, not really knowing what would come out of it.

And what happened was magical.

I manifested that $20,000 in 10 days. Yes, you read that right—10 days. And when I hit that number, I thought, If I can manifest $20K this fast, I can definitely double it. So I kept going, using the same steps I had written down. By the end of the 30-day challenge, I had manifested $41,900.

It was one of those "holy shit" moments where you realize just how powerful you really are. That experience led me to create what is now my signature viral manifestation formula, the Spark and Surrender Method™which I still teach to this day but exclusively inside my Manifestation Community - Manifest That Shit Society.

Here's the thing.

Manifestation isn't just about setting goals and hoping for the best. It's about stepping into the energy of already having what you desire. You attract what you focus on. If you're constantly focusing on lack, fear, and scarcity, then guess what? That's exactly what the Universe is going to deliver.

For example, if you're stressing about not having enough money, you're putting out scarcity energy. The Universe picks up on that and mirrors it back to you. You'll continue to face situations that reinforce your fear like random expenses popping up out of nowhere. Flat tires, broken dishwashers, unexpected bills... you name it. That's how the energy of lack keeps you stuck.

But when you shift your focus to abundance and being grateful for what you do and have then you start attracting more of it.

Even if you only have $100 in your bank account, instead of thinking, This isn't enough, you focus on, Well At least I have $100 and not negative $100. That small shift in energy sends a different signal to the Universe, which responds by bringing you more abundance.

Our entire lives are built on energy.

What you put out will always come back to you, whether it's good or bad. So, be mindful of your thoughts and emotions. You have the power to change your reality by changing your energy.

Your Turn to Manifest

I hope you've enjoyed my manifestation stories and found pieces of them you can relate to. My goal is for you to take these stories, reflect on them, and apply the lessons to your own life. Start by identifying what you want, taking aligned actions, and stepping into the version of yourself who already has what you desire.

If you need more support or want to learn exactly how to use the Spark and Surrender Method™, I invite you to join my manifestation community—**Manifest That Shit Society**. At the time of writing this book, the membership costs less than five Starbucks lattes (or whatever you coffee lovers call them—lol, I don't even drink coffee).

Inside the membership, I teach you how to create similar manifestations in your life with clarity, focus, and intention.

But here's the key thing to remember: if you don't take aligned action, nothing will change. Manifestation isn't about sitting back and waiting for magic to happen. You have to meet the Universe halfway.

Take that first step whether it's joining a community, creating a vision board, or starting a new habit and the Universe will begin to rearrange things in your favour.

I'm so excited for you to dive into the rest of this book. These stories from my students and friends are powerful examples of how manifestation can work in so many different ways. I hope you find a story that resonates with you and inspires you to keep manifesting the life you deserve.

And remember, you can always come back to this book whenever you need a boost or a reminder of your power. You've got this. The Universe is always working with you, so step into the energy of the person you want to become and watch the magic unfold.

Join the Manifest That Shit Society -www.ManifestHER.ca.

Meet The Author

Karyn Medeiros is a certified manifestation and mindset coach. She also holds the title of an international bestselling author of her first book "Manifest Like A Badass." As the founder of the Manifest *HER* brand and host of the Manifest *HER* Society, her manifestation members community and membership, Karyn empowers women worldwide through her expertise in quantum healing and manifestation.

Living in Canada with her husband and two young boys and known for her relatable and practical teaching style, Karyn connects deeply with her audience, making everyone feel like an old friend. Her podcast, "Manifest Like A Badass," blends humour and actionable wisdom, further cementing her role as a guiding force for those looking to transform their lives.

In her latest book, Karyn and her students and past clients offer readers a potent mix of personal anecdotes and expert advice, inviting them to step into their power and manifest their dreams with proof that it can be done. With her signature blend of sincerity, sass, and humour, Karyn again proves why she is a beloved coach and mentor.

MANIFEST THAT **SHIT** SOCIETY

Manifest Your **Next-Level** Self

MY MANIFESTATION COMMUNITY

Home of my viral manifestation method called **The Spark + Surrender Method**™ and **Dream Scripts**™ that students use to manifest thousands of dollars, transform into a new abundant identity and reprogram your subconscious mind.

✓ Weekly Live Lessons with manifestation coaches
✓ On-Demand Trainings
✓ Live Zoom Coaching Sessions
✓ Private Community

JOIN US AT **WWW.MANIFESTHER.CA**

MANIFEST THAT SHIT

> Sometimes, shit falls apart because something better is being built behind the scenes.

@KARYNMEDEIROS

CHAPTER 10

THE DAY WE MET SANTA CLAUS

By Amy Van Pelt

August 28, 2007, started like any other typical day for a mother of three—stressful!!! I was juggling a million things: one of my kids was sick (it seemed like one of them was always ill), and I was trying to help with some things back home with my sisters. In addition to having three daughters, I have three sisters (I'm the oldest), and they all live at least three hours away.

It had already been a rough week. One of my sisters had not been feeling well and had gotten a problematic diagnosis. While none of us were taking it well, my sister Beth (not her real name) was taking it especially hard. She was trying to be there for our sick sister since she lived the closest to her. Today was Beth's birthday, and I wanted to do something nice for her, so I ordered some flowers to be delivered to her house.

Like most young families with three small children, money was tight – almost nonexistent at times. But I ordered the flowers anyway. I used my credit card to pay for a beautiful bouquet plus the delivery fee, but I didn't consider it. I headed out the door with all three kids (ages 8, 6, & 2 for reference). We were headed to the pediatrician because, as I mentioned, one of my girls wasn't feeling well. Once we left the pediatrician's office, we headed to the pharmacy to pick up a prescription. I don't remember who was sick or what the medicine was, but that day was hot. The pharmacy's parking lot was whole, and I had to park far away from the entrance and get everyone out of the car and across the parking lot in the heat. It was brutal. I was carrying the youngest, and I remember feeling so hot, frustrated, overwhelmed, and sad (about my sister).

While waiting for the prescription, my girls looked at some Webkinz stuffed animals. I could tell they each liked one and wanted to get some, but we could not afford them. I explained they could look, but we couldn't buy anything extra now.

I noticed an older man with a short white beard looking at my girls. I couldn't tell what he was doing. It looked like he was counting them (oddly), and it made me feel uncomfortable at first. Then he motioned my girls to put the stuffed animals on the checkout counter. I politely explained that we were not planning to buy them and that my girls were just playing while we waited for our medicine. I said, "Oh, that's okay. I don't think we're going to buy them." He motioned again and then took out his wallet. That's when I realized he was planning to buy the stuffed toys for my girls. I tried to decline again, but he gently insisted. It was such a kind gesture!

I started to cry as he paid and then handed each girl the stuffed animal she had wanted. Already feeling emotional probably didn't help. I hugged him and said, "Thank you so much. That was so nice of you!" He hugged me back and replied, "You're welcome. It makes me feel good, too." I'm tearing up as I write this even now. It was such a beautiful moment. Then he turned to my girls and said, "I recently trimmed my beard. It used to be much longer." He winked and walked out of the store. That's when we stood there, realizing we had just come face to face with Santa himself.

I turned to the counter clerk, who had seen the entire interaction, and asked if he knew the man. He said, "Yes, he comes in occasionally." I asked, "Does he do this often?" He smiled and said, "Yes, quite regularly."

This unique interaction lasted only a few minutes, but I will remember it forever. On our way out of the pharmacy, we scoured the parking lot for signs of a sleigh or reindeer, but we decided they must have been keeping cool at the North Pole.

When my husband got home from work that night, I couldn't wait to tell him what had happened. As I was telling him the story, I had a full-circle moment....

As a child, I remember being told that "God will not allow himself to be outdone." My mother has always been very religious and explained to my sisters and me that God is the doer of all good things, and when we do something good, He will make sure that something equally good, if not better, will come our way. I remembered ordering the flowers for my sister that morning. I didn't have the money, so I charged them to my credit card. The total charge for the flowers plus the delivery fee was $47. What was the cost of the Webkinz that "Santa" brought for us? $49. My mind was blown! The similarity was undeniable. My mum wasn't right about everything, but when it came to understanding karma and manifesting, she hit the nail on the head.

I have chosen to live in a constant state of manifesting good things by continuously helping others. I believe we play an essential role in helping make other people's manifestations come true, and in turn, we are rewarded (by God, the Universe, Source, or whatever higher power you believe in). I have experienced numerous concrete examples that continuously support this theory.

Did I write a journal about wanting Webkinz toys for my kids? No. Did I speak it into the universe that I wanted my girls to be able to have new stuffed animals? No. Was it in my heart that I wished I could give my girls something extra in that moment as I watched them play with a stuffed elephant, cat, and penguin that we couldn't afford? Yes.

Manifesting is not only done by explicitly asking for certain things, experiences, etc. While I 100% believe it is a great way to get what you want, need, and deserve, I also think we manifest every day through our actions, the good we do, and the energy we put into the world.

A word of caution – we can't do good deeds with the intention of something good returning to us. That's not how it works. We must do good deeds for the joy and positive impact of helping someone else. Our reward often surprises us when we don't expect it, but we manifest it all the time nonetheless.

We met Santa that day. No one can tell me otherwise. I will forever be grateful for that interaction. My daughters remember it, too, and they now understand the importance of doing good for others. It will come back to you when you ask from your heart.

Meet The Author

Amy Van Pelt is a passionate advocate for personal growth and holistic well-being, residing in the scenic Hudson Valley of New York with her husband and their beloved rescue dog. With nearly three decades of life experience in this vibrant community, Amy is the proud mother of three wonderful daughters.

Holding a Master of Professional Studies in Humanistic Education, Amy has dedicated much of her adult life to higher education, where she has profoundly impacted young adults and their families. Her career has been driven by a deep commitment to nurturing the potential of others.

Amy's spiritual journey has been deeply influenced by her mother, a devout woman whose teachings on faith in God have shaped Amy's personal beliefs. Over time, Amy has come to view her spiritual path as one rooted in a deep understanding of how personal energy influences our lives and the world around us. In 2021, she became a certified Reiki Master and Chakra Crystal Energy Healer, later expanding her expertise by becoming a certified Manifestation and Mindset Coach.

One of Amy's most cherished memories is her mother's words: "God will not allow Himself to be outdone." This powerful belief—that divine forces reciprocate goodness—has inspired Amy to live a life devoted to service and manifestation. She firmly believes the universe rewards those who help others manifest their dreams.

Amy invites you to connect with her on social media (search for Amy O'Connor Van Pelt) and would love to hear from you if you discovered her through this book.

> Stop hoarding your scarcity stories. Rewrite them, shift your energy, and watch abundance pour in.

@KARYNMEDEIROS

CHAPTER 11

THE REFLECTION IN THE MIRROR: FINDING MYSELF THROUGH GRIEF, HEALING, LOVE AND MANIFESTATION

By Cindy Martel

Have you ever stared at the mirror and didn't recognize the person looking back at you? That immediate void hits like a punch to the gut, leaving you nauseated. I'll never forget that morning. I opened my eyes, expecting a day like any other. I was a mum to a beautiful 3-year-old girl, had a career I liked, and was happily married—or at least, I thought I was. Spring was in the air, and the fresh breeze slipped through the crack of a window I'd forgotten to close the night before. It was gentle, refreshing, and deceptively calm. But that day would change everything.

I stretched as I got out of bed, expecting relief, but instead, I felt nothing but aches—sharp pain in my shoulders and lower back. Strange. I walked to the washroom, splashed cold water on my face, and glanced at the mirror. That's when I saw her. The person staring back looked overwhelmed and sad. Her eyes were bloodshot, surrounded by dark circles and heavy bags. She looked tired.

There she was, a stranger in the mirror. The vibrant athlete with a big personality, the one who could light up a room and make everyone feel heard, was nowhere to be found. Instead, I was faced with someone I didn't recognize—overweight, lost, a stranger to herself. As I gazed into those unfamiliar eyes, it hit me. I whispered, 'Who are you? Where did I go?' That moment marked the beginning of my quest to rediscover her.

As I stood there, locked in a silent exchange with my reflection, I realized this wasn't just about how I looked—it was about how I felt. Somewhere along the way, I had lost myself. Life had been moving forward, but I had been standing still, weighed down by grief, uncertainty, and the heaviness of unfulfilled dreams. That moment in the mirror became my wake-up call—a turning point that led me to rediscover who I was and to manifest the life I had always dreamed of living.

I remember the moment I was first introduced to manifestation—the idea that we eat what we desire and want in life. I was a teenager, spending summer at the family cottage, but my mind was consumed with something much heavier: my strained relationship with my mother.

She had left me in the care of my grandmother and aunt when I was just eight years old. That sense of abandonment lingered, shaping the way I saw myself and the world around me.

That day at the cottage, my aunt and I decided to go for a swim. The lake was calm, almost glass-like, with barely a ripple in sight. The heat was relentless, making the air feel thick and unmoving. We floated on our air mattresses, side by side, each holding onto the corner of the other's. The gentle movement of the water rocked us in silence, and I felt at peace in that moment—utterly present. " Do you know that regardless of any circumstances you may face, you have the power to pivot, change, and create something different?" my aunt said, almost whispering. That statement left me confused. How could I believe I could have anything I wanted when I felt so profoundly abandoned? My mother had left, I had no siblings to lean on, and loneliness felt like the only constant in my life. I couldn't picture a future filled with love because, in my mind, love was something that always left.

In my mind, all I wanted was for my mother to love me and to like me enough to choose me instead of alcohol. As a teenager, I didn't understand that my mother was in pain and self-medicating. The first thing I ever manifested successfully was my mother's love. That day on the lake with my aunt, she made me breathe deeply while I closed my eyes. I remember she spoke to me for a while as I was enjoying the sun on my skin and the soft waves rocking me, bringing a sense of motherly comfort. I felt closer to God. I felt like he was listening, and I could ask anything. At that moment, I asked for my mother's love.

After that day with my aunt, I decided to put her theory to the test. Like any skeptical teenager, I questioned everything. But curiosity got the best of me, and I began manifesting small things—my grandmother's shepherd's pie for dinner, my favourite Madonna concert on VHS (remember those?), and even being picked as one of the five starters on the basketball team. And you know what? It worked! Little by little, asking for what I wanted became a habit, and I realized the transformative power of manifestation.

Then adulthood hit me. Hard.

As I grew older, I started hearing things like, "You can't always get what you want. You have to make do with what you have." Or, "Stop daydreaming. Go to work. Stay in your lane." And I listened. The weight of societal expectations and the fear of disappointment became my constant companions.

After years of struggling with infertility, I met an incredible naturopath who reintroduced me to mindfulness, meditation, and manifestation. By then, I was in my mid-30s, exhausted from life, responsibilities, disappointments, and more abandonment. It didn't take long to realize that my fear of not being a good mother had been blocking me from becoming one. With my naturopath's guidance, I began reconnecting with the 8-year-old Cindy—the little girl left behind by her mother. It took time and commitment, but I did it. I found the courage to tell my mother how I felt, and for the first time, we honestly talked. I listened. She listened. And I accepted her truth. It was the beginning of a new dynamic between us. I thought I was healed.

Around that time, I made a decision. I was going to manifest motherhood. I didn't know how it would happen—whether through adoption or by giving birth—but I knew I was ready to invite motherhood into my life. I wrote it down. I described moments with my child—playing at the park, splashing at bath time, cuddling to sleep. Every night for a whole week, I prayed. I thanked God, the Universe, for making me a mother. I spoke to my child's soul, thanking them for choosing me. I promise to always love and support them no matter what life throws at them. I started nourishing my body with better food. I was preparing, making space, welcoming the possibility of life. And I saw it—I saw myself holding my baby repeatedly.

Then, one morning in May, I took a pregnancy test.

I paced back and forth like I was in a movie, my heart racing my body feeling… different. Was it possible? After years of failed fertility treatments and tens of thousands of dollars spent, could my body have done this on its own? The answer was yes. My pregnancy went smoothly, without complications. Nine months later, my husband and I welcomed a chubby baby girl. The moment I held her, I burst with joy. I felt an overwhelming rush of love—so much that it was almost too much to hold in.

When my daughter was about six months old, I visited my hometown. There's nothing like the warmth of family to recharge your soul. One afternoon, I sat with my mother, knowing she wouldn't be with us much longer. But that day, she was happy. She laughed as she watched her only grandchild attempt to stand, wobble, fall on her little bum, and try again. I sat on the floor beside my baby, offering her my finger for support, soaking in this rare, precious moment of togetherness.

Then I noticed my mother staring. Her smile was soft, but her eyes were far away, lost in thought. She rocked gently in her chair, sipping water, looking peaceful. But her stare was so intense that I finally asked, "Mum, what is it? You've been looking at us for a while."

A summer breeze blew in from the open window, moving her hair slightly. She stopped rocking. Our eyes met, and I saw emotion surface in hers. Then she smiled, her76 voice shaking a little: "I'm so proud of the woman you've become," she said. "I wish I had been the kind of mother to you that you are to your daughter. But I want you to know—I have loved you all my life, as hard as I knew how. You are my biggest blessing, and I will always carry this love in my heart."

In that moment—over 20 years after first manifesting the love of my mother—I was finally healed.

Meet The Author

Cindy Martel is a Certified Mindset and Manifestation Coach and author of The Grief Journal: Transforming Grief into Growth. Cindy shares her unique perspective on healing through manifestation in this collaboration with Karyn, the Manifestation Queen.

Drawing on her journey of profound loss—including the passing of five family members and miscarrying twins—Cindy has turned her pain into a mission to help others heal and thrive. She founded @SoulCheckwithCindy to guide individuals through grief, helping them uncover their inner strength and create the lives they've dreamed of.

Through her coaching and work with the ManifestHer Academy, Cindy empowers others to embrace authenticity, resilience, and joy. Passionate about the human condition, her travels have taught her invaluable lessons about connection and inner strength. She is also devoted to her daughter, whom she was blessed with after years of fertility challenges—a manifestation she treasures deeply.

Her story shows how growth can emerge from even the darkest moments. Cindy believes healing begins when we honour our emotions, set clear intentions, and manifest purposefully.

Follow Cindy on Instagram at @SoulCheckwithCindy to learn more and start your manifestation journey.

MANIFEST THAT SHIT

The Universe loves a confident badass.

@KARYNMEDEIROS

CHAPTER 12

STARS, SIGNS, AND SECOND CHANCES

By Helen Meredith

February 2020

A few weeks before the world goes into lockdown.

Lying in the darkness, a single tear rolls down my cheek. Turning over, I glance at the clock: it's 4 a.m. It's been another sleepless night, and I feel utterly exhausted. Going to work in just a few hours weighs heavily on me. I quietly get out of bed, wiping the flowing tears with the back of my hand as I go downstairs.

From the window, I look up at the starry sky. It is a cold, crisp winter night, the sky scattered with stars shining brightly like diamonds. I feel a shiver and pull my dressing gown tightly around me against the cool air of the still house. My heart aches, my soul aches. Staring upwards to the sky through teary eyes, I whisper to The Universe, 'I have no idea how this will play out; I just know I can no longer go on like this. Physically and mentally, I am done; something must change. I trust and know that somehow this will all work out.'

Here I am, aged 54, in the dead of night, making a life-altering decision. I'm writing a resignation letter to my employer. I feel I have no choice; I am burned out…My health has become a real source of anxiety for me. These days, I no longer recognize the reflection of the girl staring back at me in the mirror. I feel as though I've lost myself completely. It feels utterly overwhelming; I'm scared. I know dropping to one household salary will pressure my relationship with my husband. Yet I know that I have reached the point where something must give. I cannot go on like this for my physical health and sanity.

I go to work and hand in my notice to my manager. We have a family ski trip booked for the following week. She asked me to reconsider my decision while on holiday as she values my work and wants me to stay. I agree to take that week to consider it. My heart knows what my answer will be.

The news on TV reports of a virus sweeping across the world. Something that just a couple of months earlier seemed so far away. We are advised that travelling and heading off to Italy is safe. On reflection, I don't know how I managed to ski those first couple of days, as I was feeling so exhausted. We were informed that Italy went onto red alert the second day of the holiday and would close its borders within a few hours. Twelve hours later, we are across the border in Austria, awaiting a specially chartered aircraft to bring us back to the UK. It was such an eerie experience. Upon returning, there are new rules, and we are advised to stay in quarantine for 14 days. A few days later, the UK went into complete lockdown, and the world we knew changed overnight.

I never did go back to my job. A few weeks later, a letter arrived from the Health Authority informing me that I was at a very high risk of being hospitalized from the virus. I am advised to isolate myself from other members of the household, no hugs, no eating together. It felt like my whole world had just crumbled around me. My anxiety goes off the scale, resulting in my health suffering further. Looking back at those long months seems like a blur to me now.

Coming out of the lockdown, my confidence was at an all-time low, and I had slipped even further into that feeling of losing myself. Slowly, over the months, I have piled on the pounds. Having always been active, my body feels so alien to me now. I ask myself, Is this it? Is this what it feels like to be getting older? Will I ever find a way back to the vibrant girl I used to be?....

Nature has always soothed my soul, so I started taking daily walks in the country lanes where I live. Stopping to observe and enjoy the beautiful wildlife around me, these moments of mindfulness while walking became the one thing I would look forward to every day. Often listening to a podcast, I set about my research into health and wellness for midlife women. Looking back, it is my gut instinct nudging me. There was a missing piece to the puzzle as to why my health had declined; it became my mission to look after my body and find ways to get back to full health again. One evening, while walking, I listened to a podcast interview with a lady telling her story of her struggles with her health in midlife. It stopped me in my tracks! Her story was identical to mine…her symptoms were all being driven by her hormones. The relief I felt I could not explain was that I wasn't going crazy! There was a reason I was feeling this way. My hormones were on a roller-coaster, leaving me with countless symptoms. I was in perimenopause!

A few months after seeking help from a menopause specialist, I began to feel a little more like my old self. My sleep started to improve, and feelings of joy for the simple things in my life returned. I spend time on Instagram researching and following all things health and wellness. When I encountered a lady running a Menopause Support Coach Certification, my inner voice nudged me again…. I enrolled in the course, put my head down, and began my studies of all things menopause and midlife. It was the first shoot of growth for positive change.

We are on a break at our favourite place, Newport in Pembrokeshire in West Wales, a couple of weeks later—a land of ancient burial grounds where the famous Stonehenge Bluestones originated. Walking alone around the quiet beach, I noticed a large driftwood set way back up from the shoreline. I am drawn to it and decide to look, maybe sit for a while. As I approach the driftwood, I notice something different. At one end, someone has sketched the most beautiful image of a woman's face. She is smiling; the image is quite magical. As I sit peacefully watching the gentle waves lapping the water's edge, I glance behind me and notice something tucked in a crevice. It is tucked on the far side of the driftwood. Taking it in my hand, I recognize it as a gratitude pebble. Painted on it is an image of a bee. In beautiful writing, a simple message…. 'Bee Happy'…. I catch my breath. It's a sign…. I was meant to sit on that driftwood log that day, but then the time came to find 'my happiness' again.

The weeks go by…. While researching on Instagram, I came across a fantastic lady named Joan Macdonald. I am amazed and fascinated by her story. She is in her mid-seventies and looks incredible! At seventy, suffering from many health symptoms, her daughter, a bodybuilder, takes her mum under her wing and begins this fantastic transformation. It was a light bulb moment for me. If this lady could do this, what would be my excuse? Following Joan on Instagram, the algorithm throws up accounts of other midlife women, changing the narrative around aging. Back then, I had no idea about the extraordinary friendship and support network that would develop with some of these women. That's the power of manifesting and energies coming together!

I begin to apply what I am learning about nutrition, movement, and mindfulness to my daily life. Slowly, little by little, I began to feel my confidence return. September 2022 comes, and I graduate as a certified Menopause Support Coach. I feel so proud of myself and feel a significant positive shift in my energy. Around this time, I began to see the word 'Gratitude' everywhere; I have always considered myself grateful. However, there always seemed to be a condition to my gratitude… 'As soon as X Y Z happens, I will feel happy.' Intrigued, I began to look further into gratitude and manifestation. There, I find the same recurring theme. The more grateful you are for what you already have, the more abundance will flow through to you.

In the Summer of 2022, I will begin a daily gratitude journal practice. Every morning, I write in my journal about the things I am grateful for, big or small. Then, in the evening, just before bedtime, I would hold the gratitude pebble in my palm, closing my eyes, reflecting on the positive things that had happened that day. The more consistent I was with my practice, the more I felt a fundamental shift in my energy, and my days would play out much more positively.

In my quest to get healthier, I joined a fitness app that September. I observed the other ladies progressing in strength training for a few months. I guess that little niggling doubt, you know, that self-talk, telling you, 'It's only for other women. How do I even start?' My inner voice nudges me again, saying, 'You just need to show up and do what you can.' On 6th January, 2023, I did just that. At first, it felt super hard on some days. However, the community inside the app spurred me on. Within 6 weeks of being consistent, I had lost a few pounds and felt my energy levels improving.

A 6-week challenge starts on 1st March, and I signed up. As part of that program, I am to send progress pictures; these were to have something for comparison after the six weeks. I remember feeling physically sick; I took a deep breath and pressed the button to start the challenge. By the end of the 6 weeks, there was a noticeable difference in my body, energy, and mindset. As part of the program, I was lucky to speak with Joan and her daughter on Zoom. I will never forget Joan saying, ' You look beautiful now anyway' as we wrapped up our conversation. I clung so tightly to those words of kindness. Words have such power; they can be the key to unlocking the self-belief potential that someone has buried deep inside their unconscious mind.

By August, I plucked up the courage to apply to work with a 1:1 fitness coach. The coach is Canadian, and I am drawn to her energy when I come across her on Instagram. I apply alongside hundreds of other women. My heart and soul go into that application. I got shortlisted for a Zoom call/interview with her. The meeting was scheduled for 1 am UK time, wanting it so severely that interview timing was irrelevant to me. The meeting went well; the emails would be sent within a few days. I visualized the email popping into my messages. Imagining myself opening that email.... Congratulations Helen! Over and over, I rehearsed how it would feel. The excitement! Pure joy! Two days later, that very email appeared in my inbox! And so the next phase began, manifesting a healthy, strong body.

My start date was early December; everyone thought I was crazy to start before Christmas. I plucked up the courage to go into a gym for the first time to do my initial workout on the program. With Caroline's help over those months, my courage and confidence flourished. The new year arrives, I am feeling pretty good, my newfound habits support my body.... It's like something magical is happening. As well as working hard, I make complete peace with my body. My gratitude practice had begun to flow into all aspects of my life. This, I believe, is key to my successful transformation. I learned to love my body as it was, being grateful for everything it does for me. I swear that was the secret sauce that allowed my body to shed excess energy—the energy I had been carrying in those extra pounds on my body for a very long time.

My fitness coach is super organized and suggests I get a planner to schedule my workouts. When it arrives, I open the cover. The first page is titled 'My Dreams.' As I wrote the list on February 19, 23, I let my imagination run free; after all, it did say it was a dream list! Some key things I wrote down that manifested still blow my mind today! Here are a few of those things....

A retreat in Canada...... I met my coach, Caroline, in person and some of the ladies from the fitness group in Toronto (fall 2023.) Here's the thing: the retreat was due in Whistler that fall. I felt so disappointed as I knew it was a little out of my reach. Then, out of the blue, in mid-summer, the venue was changed to Toronto. I had written on that dream list: Go to Toronto and, on the following line, meet Caroline in person! I had written it down, and it manifested. I couldn't quite believe it!

Also on my list, I had written that I wanted to meet Pam and Emmie in real life (two ladies I connected with at the beginning of my fitness journey). I also wrote to meet Joan McDonald in person. Joan is a Canadian now living in Mexico. For a few weeks leading up to my trip to Toronto, I felt I would get to meet Joan when I was there. Around 10 days before I fly out, Joan plans a trip back to Toronto. Yes, you guessed it, I met her and Pam! I got to meet Emmie just a few months later.

Do a photoshoot in Toronto.

This was another dream.... I did get to do a photoshoot to celebrate my fitness transformation. After the shoot, I saw myself in a new light!

I surpassed all my expectations and manifested a fit, more muscular body, losing 40lbs (total loss from Jan 2022 -April 2023). I finally felt like the fitter, healthier version of my previous self.

Go to King Charles III's Coronation in London

Despite being one of the busiest weekends in London's history, three friends and I managed to find accommodation and get a bird' s-eye view of the procession on The Mall, just down from Buckingham Palace!

Get a Robin to eat out of my hand.

The Robin is the UK's favourite bird. We have a couple that feed in my garden, and I often thought of how I would love to feed one out of my hand. In January 2024, I noticed one on the ground outside. I went out, and although he looked unharmed, this little Robin did not fly off as I approached him. I gently scooped him up in my hands and brought him inside. Immediately, he curls up tight as though in a nest. I held him cradled in my hands for around 40 minutes. When he wakes, he looks at me. I called my husband to get a little bird food and some water. That little guy fed out of my hand for another 15 minutes or so. He then happily jumped onto the back of my hand, looking around. I gently stood to take him outside. He looked at me with his head on the side, and we exchanged a few moments; it was pretty magical! Once outside, he flies onto my garden fence and sits there, looking back at me as if to say thank you again before flying away.

To meet Joan McDonald in Mexico

Yes, this also manifests. In March 2024, I fly to Tulum, Mexico, for a retreat organized by Pam. The retreat is themed around women supporting women. It was the most magical time of connection and relaxation.

Coldwater swims with the girls

I chuckled when I put this on the list…How was this going to be possible? We are scattered worldwide, one in Toronto, one in Mexico, and the other on Vancouver Island. However, we do get to have that cold-water swim during the retreat. The underground waters of the Mexican cenotes are very refreshing and very cold! The colour of the water, the rock formations, and the pure magic of experiencing this with my beautiful friends was something else!

2024, as it turned out, was one of the most magical and unique years to date. On returning from my trip to Mexico, I reflect on the Vision Board I created in January. It features a yoga retreat and a picture of Twiggy (a pet name the girls have for me after my photoshoot in Toronto). I realize, wow, yes, I got to do another photoshoot in a magical cenote with the fantastic ladies on the retreat. Also, a picture of a group of women's hands is in a circle on the board. I went to my phone and pulled up the photos from the trip. On the final day of the retreat, one of the ladies kindly gifted us all a bracelet; I remember someone called me over to put my hand in a circle to take a photograph. Back at home, I am looking at that identical picture I placed on my vision board in January!

Throughout 2024, I will hone in and focus on my gratitude practice. Every morning, I stand barefoot on the grass, watching the sunrise and feeling grateful for everything I have. It's a time when I quietly check in with myself, genuinely listening and noticing the subtle nuances and gut feelings we often miss in the busyness of life. Looking up at the vastness of the sky, I ask for a clear sign to help me understand the path I am currently on - where I need to be and what direction I should take. All the while, I visualize the things I want to create and bring into my life.

Afterward, I sit with my gratitude journal; putting my thoughts onto paper is a powerful tool. Writing about what I am grateful for, how I would like my day to go, and what I would like to call in and manifest is essential to my practice. I then spend a few minutes writing about my ideal life, immersing myself in so much detail like a child with a vivid imagination! Doing both of these practices sets me up for the day. Then I surrender my requests and wait to see what magical gifts arrive from the Universe.

I sometimes need to pinch myself when I think of the amazing people and opportunities I have had in the past two years. It just blows my mind! I have incredible, like-minded friends, outstanding mentors, and collaborations with wonderful people. Practicing gratitude has completely changed my life. It took me from complete burnout to thriving and pursuing my dreams. I am truly grateful!

Where attention goes, energy flows. When you change your energetic vibration, you really can change your life!

All the love

Helen Findme at Helen MeredithWellness Coaching @helenmeredith.com On Instagram @ perfectly_imperfect_fit

Meet The Author

Helen Meredith is a certified Menopause Support Coach and a Manifestation and Mindset Coach who combines a deep passion for holistic health with a wealth of expertise in personal transformation. With a background in the aviation industry as an Air Cabin Crew member, Helen thrived in the vibrant atmospheres of cities like Dubai and London, embracing the energy and excitement of diverse cultures. However, when midlife arrived, unexpected challenges caused a disconnection from her true self. She navigated this transformative period through resilience and determination, emerging as a stronger, more self-assured version of herself.

Now residing in the picturesque landscapes of Wales, Helen is deeply rooted in nature, which serves as her anchor. She enjoys hiking, yoga, weight training, and reading—practices that nurture her physical and mental well-being. A proud mother to a 23-year-old son, she is also happily married. Helen is passionate about empowering midlife women navigating menopause, challenging outdated and harmful narratives around aging, and rewriting the story of what it means to grow older. Alongside an inspiring community of women in their 50s, 60s, and 70s, she advocates for the belief that midlife is not the end but rather a new and exciting beginning.

As a mindset coach, Helen helps women harness the power of their thoughts and beliefs to manifest their desired lives. She recognizes the beautiful potential in every woman, even when they can't see it themselves. Together, they celebrate this next chapter, embrace the journey, and redefine what it means to thrive in midlife—unlocking incredible possibilities

> Get up, shift your vibe, and claim what's yours.

@KARYNMEDEIROS

CHAPTER 13

AWAKENING POTENTIAL: A WOMAN'S JOURNEY OF RESILIENCE, EMPOWERMENT AND MANIFESTATION.

By Jana Taglianetti

Manifestation for me has spanned throughout decades of my life. I was first introduced to this concept when I read the book You Can Heal Your Life by Louise Hay. It was the early to mid-90s, and I was in college. I had just failed out-of-state school. I was a biology major, and even though I knew the general direction I wanted to be in science, I did not know what to do. I enrolled in a community college to fix my grades and applied to nursing school at the urging of one of my professors. The healthcare field has always surrounded me. My grandfather was a doctor. My grandmother was a nurse. My father was a dentist. My aunt was a nurse. My uncle was a pharmacist. Nursing fit the direction that I wanted to go in. I was working a job in Manhattan and wavering about what I was doing with my life. My cousin Stella had given me the book You Can Heal Your Life and urged me to read it. Not only did I read it, but I also started implementing visualization techniques outlined in the book. It completely changed how I thought of myself, changed my mindset, and made me realize that anything was possible.

I began to visualize getting into nursing school. I visualized the phone call; I visualized what the conversation would be; I visualized myself signing up for class living on campus; I visualized it all. By the end of the summer, I received notice that I made it into nursing school. That summer, visualizing getting into nursing school wasn't the only thing that I was manifesting that was coming to fruition. I started to be able to think of conversations, and then they would happen. I began to be able to know things before they happened. A different world was opening up to me.

I was in nursing school for about two years and spent my last semester doing a clinical at home at a prominent New York City hospital. Continuing my visualization and manifestation techniques, I started to visualize passing the New York State nursing boards, landing my first nursing job, and manifesting a boyfriend in my personal life.

Life was everything I had wanted it to be, everything I had visualized and manifested. However, I had stopped practicing manifestation because I thought that was it. I had what I wanted but didn't see the big picture.

I was working as a nurse for about two years. My boyfriend, Marvin, and I had an apartment together. All of the manifestations and visualizations had come true. I thought that I was set. I had a job, an apartment, and a boyfriend, and we lived life to the fullest. Then, I got pregnant, and in 2003 we had a daughter. Marvin lost his first job. I continued to work two jobs while I was pregnant. Before she was born, we moved into a townhome closer to our parents. Marvin did get another job and continued to look for better work. In 2010, we got married, and in 2012, we welcomed our second daughter.

Throughout our relationship and marriage, Marvin jumped from job to job as I struggled to pay the bills, care for the kids, and keep our family together. Many arguments ensued throughout our relationship, with the common denominator of finances or lack thereof. He did not financially contribute to the mortgage, house bills, groceries, kids' activities, or anything else. I was the sole provider. The majority of our arguments were about finances. I was stuck in a cycle and did not know how to break free. I was losing myself. I did not recognize myself anymore. I felt like a robot just going through the motions of daily life to keep it together. The more I tried, the more I tried to help Marvin get his life together for himself and his family, the worse it got. I didn't understand it. I didn't know why he was not the provider, the husband, or the father I knew he had the potential to be. I failed to realize I was not dealing with a standard, logical situation.

In 2012, while on maternity leave, I was at the beginning of the next five-year cycle I would've never seen coming. I had a newborn baby, and if that weren't life-changing enough, my life would be flipped upside down. My grandmother, my father's mother, would subsequently die at the age of 91 after a very brief illness. My uncle, my godfather, my father's brother, suddenly became ill, was diagnosed with lung cancer, and within six months succumbed to cancer and passed away. Overlapping this, my mother became sick. The breast cancer that she had beat 19 years before had come back in her liver, and there started a three-year battle. That was happening; my other grandmother, my mother's mother, who I was extremely close to, passed away at the age of 100. My best girlfriend was diagnosed with a rare form of cancer, and after a grueling treatment, she is healthy and in remission.

My mother, my best friend, fought a 3-year battle and, in 2016, passed away at home. She died on October 19, 2016, and her burial was on October 24, my 41st birthday.

We were all devastated. My father became a different person during that period. He was angry and deeply saddened. He and my mother had been dating since they were 14 and knew no other life without her in it. I managed him; my older daughter was in eighth grade, I had a toddler, and Marvin had no job. I was the nurse manager of a local hospital's pre- and post-op units. The stress was overwhelming, and after her death, I became completely numb. My marriage was spiraling. I was doing my best to be a good mother for my girls, putting on a happy face, but on the inside, there was nothing.

In February 2018, my first lightbulb moment came from the most unlikely source: my accountant. I have known my accountant, Dennis, for over 20 years. And this one particular time that I went to file my taxes, he looked at me over his desk, dead in my eyes, and said Jana, what the fuck are you doing? At first, I was taken aback. What do you mean? I thought something was wrong with my taxes. He looked at me and said you have worked consistently the same job for years and only left your job for a better opportunity. You just handed me your taxes, and Marvin has seven W-2 forms in one year. What are you doing?

This was the first time an outsider, just looking at the paper, could pinpoint and shake me into reality. I knew that my marriage was a mess, I knew that I was stuck in a cycle, and I realized that at that moment, the only person that was going to get me out of it was me.

The following day, I washed my face in the bathroom. I looked at myself in the mirror and said, "What are you doing?" I started talking to myself in the mirror because I didn't recognize myself. The me 20 years ago was driven, knew what she wanted, and didn't let anything stand in the way of getting it. How did I let myself get to this moment?

This is where I started to make the change. I started talking to myself daily in the mirror and tapping into muscle memory, visualization, and a manifestation I hadn't used in years. I said, "I am worthy," and repeated this daily. This was the beginning of my positive daily affirmations.

I gave myself a timeline, a deadline, so to speak. If the status of our relationship, his getting a job, and my overall happiness did not change and improve by the end of summer, Labour Day, I was finally going to pull the trigger and file for divorce.

In March 2018, the fog started to lift. I began to find my confidence through another unlikely source. A high school friend I had reconnected with on social media was selling makeup through a network marketing company. I needed the extra money and liked that this was a flexible opportunity. I didn't realize this was the beginning of finding my confidence, and unimaginable doors were opened for me. I signed up with her, and through this business, I met Karyn. I truly believe the Universe brought this all together.

The summer went by, and it was not a good one. He was not working. I would take my older daughter to a national bowling tournament every July. This particular year, the tournament was held in Dallas, Texas. Marvin and I spoke about it, and he was going to stay home and do a project in the house we had been talking about, painting the living room and hallway. Our house was tiny, so this project could've been completed in a few days. I went to Dallas with my older daughter, my younger daughter, and my father. The tournament is a week long. Attending these tournaments is by no means a vacation. It's every day spent in a bowling alley with minimal time to relax. It is exhausting, to say the least. You can understand if you have ever travelled to a tournament with your child's sports team.

When we returned, I walked into a mess. Dirty dishes were piled in the sink, and painting supplies and clothes were all over the kitchen and living room. It looked and smelt like a fraternity house. The project was nowhere near completion. He had taped off the molding, removed the light fixtures and switch covers, etc., and that was it. I had to return to work the next day. I immediately began cleaning the kitchen, unpacking, and doing laundry, and then I finally snapped and said something. I remember the moment clearly as day. I was standing at the kitchen sink, and he was lying on the couch. I wasn't yelling, but my tone was heard. I conveyed the utter disrespect I felt. The project was not completed, and the house was in disarray. He had time to go out with his friends and post it on social media, but he didn't have time to do what he needed for his family.

He completely ignored me from that day until September—the silent treatment. For two and a half months, he did not acknowledge my existence. I still paid the bills, went to work, cared for the kids, and cared for the house. He lived off the food I bought, lived under the roof I paid the mortgage for, watched the television I paid for, and used the cell phone I paid for, but he did not speak one word to me.

My last straw was when my cousin (and best friend) Stella told me about her conversation with my older daughter. My older daughter spent Labour Day weekend at my cousin's house. My cousin asked her how things were going, and my daughter unloaded on her. She continued telling my cousin how she watched me work, care for her younger sister, care for the house, cook dinner, and clean while "he" did nothing. He slept on the couch most of the day. He wouldn't when I asked him to do something, even if it was for them. She watched and heard us fight. That was when I realized that not allowing my daughters to grow up thinking that our life, our marriage, was how life was supposed to be. It wasn't. It wasn't a healthy relationship. My daughters were witnessing all of it, and I did not want them to have our dysfunctional relationship as their model of what love and happiness were.

In September 2018, I told Marvin I wanted a divorce. That two-and-a-half months of complete silence was a blessing. It gave me clarity. I knew this would be one of the most challenging periods of my life, but I also knew that if I did not break the cycle, it would continue.

In March 2019, I officially filed for divorce, and for the next year, I lived a living hell. Filled with a divorce trial, multiple orders of protection against him, violations of those orders, torture, and torment. The best and only way I could describe it to people is that it was like detaching a parasite from its host.

It was finally over on March 16, 2020, the day the world shut down in the largest pandemic in a century. I was finally divorced.

I came back to my roots of visualization and manifestation. My house was in shambles through years of neglect of either not having the money and/or Marvin and I making a plan but never being able to execute it due to finances. There were so many projects to be done, but I did not know how to do it. I created a vision board; I put pictures of a redone bathroom, a finished basement, a vacation for my kids and me, and everything I wanted and needed to get done. My goal was to finish the projects in my house, and when my younger daughter graduated the fifth grade, sell it and move to New Jersey. I had wanted to move to New Jersey since my older daughter was in eighth grade; however, life had gotten in the way then. Now was the time to do what I had always dreamt of: giving my girls a better life.

Through practicing positive affirmation manifestations, getting a lot of guidance from Karyn, self-help, videos, podcasts, and coaches, my manifestations on that vision board became a reality one by one. Through my self-healing, I learned that I was married to a narcissist and was a survivor of a narcissistic marriage.

In late April 2023, I put the for-sale sign in front of my house. I manifested my next steps. I wanted a three-bedroom townhouse with a basement and a garage. The main bedroom had a walk-in closet and a bathroom. I placed four different bids on houses, but they all fell through. The summer proved tumultuous, not having a place to live until 2 days before I closed on the sale of my house. However, the universe pulled through. I landed in the most fantastic part of New Jersey. Although I don't own my townhome, it is precisely what I requested. My younger daughter is flourishing in her new school and has made new friends. The area we live in is peaceful. My older daughter continues to get her master's degree in education and bowls for an NCAA Division 1 Women's collegiate bowling team. We are happy and blessed.

Throughout my journey, I have realized that manifestation is not a one-time deal. It's a progression, a way of life.

I am now a Certified Mindset & Manifestation Coach, and my mission is to help other women realize their full potential.

I am continuing my path of visualization and manifestation because I know this is just a pit stop on my life journey.

MANIFEST THAT SHIT

Meet The Author

Jana Taglianetti, RN, is a transformational Mindset and Manifestation Coach who empowers individuals to overcome their limitations and architect the life they envision. Drawing on her nursing and personal development background, she creates a unique coaching experience that blends practical strategy with spiritual wisdom.

As the innovator behind the Pen It & Purge It Method, Jana has guided countless clients through identifying and releasing deeply held limiting beliefs. This groundbreaking approach has catalyzed profound personal transformation, helping individuals clear the path toward their most authentic aspirations.

Understanding the power of daily practice, Jana developed the Self-Love and Money Mindset Positive Daily Affirmation Cards. This powerful tool helps users rewire their thinking patterns and cultivate an abundance mindset that attracts personal fulfillment and financial prosperity.

Jana's coaching philosophy centres on believing that every individual possesses untapped potential waiting to be unleashed. Through her workshops, one-on-one coaching sessions, and innovative tools, she creates a supportive environment where clients discover their inner strength and learn to manifest their dreams with intention and purpose.

Connect with Jana: Facebook: @Jana Tags Instagram: @janataglianettiRN TikTok: @JanaTagsRN

Use this QR code to access my website

JanaTaglianetti.com

Visualize your success so vividly that even your haters start seeing it.

@KARYNMEDEIROS

CHAPTER 14

EMBRACING THE MAGIC OF TRUST

By Jennifer Smith

The day I dropped off my eldest daughter at college was a mix of emotions I never expected. I was so excited for her to start her journey into adulthood and for me to watch her spread her wings and fly. I was honestly not expecting to feel the heartbreak, devastation, and a sense of being abandoned that came once I was on that plane flying home. I struggled with leaving her in the big city all by herself. How can I leave her when I have been here to protect her for the last 20 years? This would be my new regular, and I did not like it.

When I returned home, my house felt so quiet; no more singing or music came from her room. No more late-night chat or coffee runs in the morning. We are both morning people, sharing our stories every morning. I felt the loneliness creep in, grieving this like a loss. Not just a physical loss but also a loss of my existence for the last 20 years. I remember standing in the doorway of my daughter's bedroom, still and silent, wondering what my new role would be like.

I started to experience some health issues along the way: a racing heart waking me up at night, complete panic attacks during the day, and also waking me up at night in terror. After a few weeks of this, I thought I must be dying. I can't live like this anymore. I did not want to harm myself, but I also did not know how I could keep on living like this, in complete despair. I contacted my doctor, who had a fantastic conversation about reframing my thoughts. It was difficult, and I still felt lost, but that sparked something in me. I had spent so much time helping my children grow that I had forgotten my growth. It was meant to be this way; I am very proud of dedicating my life to my kids. It was everything to me. And I would not change a single day.

I dropped my daughter off at college, and at Christmas time, my kids had given me a gratitude journal. One morning, I said to myself that I had reached the bottom; I was depressed and felt zero hope for myself. What is one thing I could do, just one little thing that I could do everyday to get me out of this hell hole of ruminating thoughts, depression, and anxiety? I decided to write inward in this gratitude journal to see what happens.

I have written down daily gratitudes off and on in the years before, but nothing consistent enough to see or feel the magic. I knew that magical vibration was out there,

but I did not believe it was for me; it was only for other people. I needed to trust, but I was not there yet. I started to think about what dreams I had put on hold. What passions had I never explored?

I was mostly terrified to confront the question: WHO AM I NOW?

MANIFEST THAT SHIT

On January 1, 2024, I committed to writing in my lovely new gratitude journal. I told myself, "Just write in it and see what happens." By day 5 of writing, all the pages kept falling out on each one I had written on. I thought to myself, is this a sign to stop? Is this a sign of letting go? I continued writing, but the pages kept falling. I emailed the company to let them know, and they immediately sent me a new one, with apologies. I felt, hmmm, did I just manifest that? I usually meet with resistance when making a complaint.

I continued writing, with pages falling out. I felt like this was an old friend, and I did not want to throw away all the pages that held so much for me. Within 2 weeks, I woke up one morning, writing in my journal, and realized I was feeling something. What was that feeling? It felt like a veil had lifted, and I recognized what it was. It was hope. It was the first morning in months I had felt anything other than doom and gloom. Could this be happening? Like never before, I cried so grateful for this daily writing and how it was helping give life back to me in so many ways. I started recognizing little things going my way, like the publishing company sending me a new journal, parking spots being available wherever I was driving, and tiny nudges from the universe whispering, "Keep going." So I did.

In that third week of journaling my gratitude, I also decided to write a daily affirmation. I chose I AM OPEN TO NEW ADVENTURES. I had no clue what adventures I wanted; travelling, of course, has always been a top dream of mine. I did not want to control this, though. I laid down my shield of protection, control, and fear for the first time. I finally permitted myself to be open and TRUST what the universe had in store for me. The freedom to follow the breadcrumbs the Universe laid down for me.

The breadcrumbs started to fall, and I picked up the first one 5 days after writing my new intention. I was scrolling on social media when I came across a post from Karyn. She posted that she was opening up a new training program at her Manifest. Her Academy to become a Certified Manifestation and Mindset Coach. Before I continued, I had not seen Karyn on my algorithm for a long time; she was on my timeline for a reason. I immediately messaged her to get more information. Before I got that information, I knew this was for me. I did not need the info. I started giggling; this is what I do with nervous energy. It is fantastic but also a curse, depending on where you are. If you know, you know. I was signed up within 48 hours.

I felt so excited, something I had not thought about for a long time. After putting my life on hold for 20-something years raising children, could this be it? Could this be the stepping stone to a life I desired? Something that was just for me? I had had those feelings that would pop in randomly, questioning if motherhood was it for me—all those emotions and questioning dissipated once I signed up for the training. A Deeper feeling of hope began to come forward, and I knew this was a turning point for me.

I never once doubted my decision, not even a thought of quitting, which had a running loop in my mind on many other occasions of signing up for a class. I felt fearful, but I didn't know why. In hindsight, I think My soul knew I was about to let everything go that had held me back my entire life, breaking free from the chains I had put on myself. All the limiting beliefs were going to be no longer. A surrender to trust. It was on a level I did not even understand yet.

Once I started the classes, I expressed how nervous and scared I was. I took a deep breath and was utterly committed to it. I promised myself not to give up on myself, as I had done many times before. I wanted to show up fully, be open with my experiences, ask questions, and be present. I am so proudly stuck with this commitment. Let me tell you what an experience I started to have.

As I began applying the principles of manifestation and mindset shifts in my life, I witnessed incredible changes in what I was achieving, how I was feeling, and how the energy in my household was changing. It slowly took hold of each member of my family. My husband began to write in a gratitude journal and followed along with my training, being my first practice student. We were now witnessing growth together. We started to connect again on a level of partnership. When you are in the throes of parenting, the husband/wife relationship can take a hit. So, feeling this connection and starting to grow from a place of two adults who can support each other has been fantastic. It felt like a rebirth of our marriage was unfolding, dusting off that old energy and flying out together, learning as we grew.

I had struggled all through my years of staying home with my kids. Even though my husband and I had agreed before we had kids that I would stay home, I could not get past the fact that I would not have my own money. Some days, it left me feeling lesser than, and it took many years to resolve that what I was doing was way better than what money could ever offer me. With this being said, once I was in the midst of the training, I had been super curious: as a stay-at-home mum and homeschooler, how would I manifest money? Travel? Opportunities? After all, don't they require money? Where will that money come from if you make zero dollars a year? I told you I was starting from the bottom. I remained in that curious state, trusting it would come. I did not once try to control the outcome. I would typically start looking for a way to earn money, scrambling to make it happen. Not this time. Well, let me tell you, the money has begun to flow. I'll never forget the first time I realized that the money I would manifest would come through my husband.

I planned to pick up a planter from college in spring 2024. There was a musical I had wanted to see while there, but would you know it, it was ending before we could make it down. In the meantime, my 12-year-old son was texting me that a show he was dying to see would take place the same weekend in the city I would be in. I laughed to myself; this kid will manifest all of us going. Within the week, my daughter told me they also extended the musical we wanted to attend. What is happening?! Could this be the Universe rearranging everything to work out in our favour? I asked my husband if we could all go away that weekend to move my daughter, see the musical the truck shows my son wanted to see, and bring my daughter home. Sadly, the answer was no. We did not have the money. I was devastated only for a minute. Then I told him, I am going to manifest it. So it did. I wrote down exactly what I wanted, and by Sunday of that week, my husband walked in the door to tell me that he received the money he had been owed, and we could now all go to Toronto! We had the best time: we went to Niagara Falls, we saw the musical, we saw the truck show, we moved my daughter into the apartment she manifested in, and we ALL came back home together.

This solidified my belief in manifesting my dream life. Why are we not doing this if we can manifest and create anything? The ball was rolling, and extra money was coming in through my husband. Not only did we manifest the trip to Toronto, but also a dream trip to California, Florida, and back to Toronto. All within 5 months. I felt like I was dreaming. Was this happening to me? Yes, it was. I was tired from all the travel and needed a rest. I had been talking to my daughter and asked if she was ready to travel again. She said YES. I said, I am, too! It's time to start manifesting my 2025 trips. At the beginning of 2024, I told myself I wanted three visits this year. We took 4. So, for 2025, I would like three trips again; I said the universe. My family loves Disney; the kids ask if we can return to Florida or California. I said I was tired of going there. How about Disney Paris? I wanted to know if we would ever get there, but why not put it out there?

This past Christmas, my mum sat down and told us to close our eyes; she had a surprise for us. What the heck can it be? Maybe a new vacuum? We opened our eyes, and she made little posters. The first was a picture of a plane, the next a picture of the Eiffel Tower, and now a picture of Disneyland Paris. She was paying for us to go to Paris, France. I passed out after that. We were all in shock. My husband and I just looked at each other, crying. He looked white as a ghost. Even my kids were quiet, in disbelief. We are going to Paris! After the shock wore off, it took a few days to realize what had just happened.

What had just happened was that my mum gave me this amazing gift of travel to Paris and this fantastic gift from the universe.

I deserve the gift of believing in myself again. I create a fantastic life by changing my mindset and aligning my intentions, energy, and actions to produce lasting results.

This journey has taught me that transformation isn't about perfection. It is about progress, self-awareness, and learning to trust the process. Never give up on yourself. I am so grateful to live with purpose, confidence, and alignment.

Meet The Author

Jennifer Smith is a Canadian stay-at-home mum, homeschooler, and empty nester who embraces life's next chapter as her teens and young adults become independent. Married to her best friend and the proud mum of three incredible children, Jennifer has spent years cultivating a life centred around family, love, and personal growth. As her children venture into adulthood, she is navigating the beautiful balance between giving them space to grow and continuing to be a source of support and guidance.

Beyond her role as a mother, Jennifer is passionate about travel and adventure. She believes that experiencing new places and cultures enriches her life and the lives of her family. This adventurous spirit fuels her journey and shapes her approach to coaching and her work as an Intuitive Energy Reader.

As a Manifestation & Mindset Coach, Jennifer is on a mission to help women—mainly stay-at-home mums and empty nesters—rediscover their power and unlock the potential within themselves. She has seen firsthand how transformative mindset shifts and deep gratitude can radically change one's life. Through her coaching, Jennifer empowers women to break free from self-imposed limitations and the societal expectations that often hold them back.

Jennifer's approach is grounded in the belief that it's never too late to create the life you've always dreamed of. She inspires her clients to trust themselves, embrace their inner strength, and take bold, inspired action toward their goals—whether launching a new career, embarking on a personal journey, or simply learning to prioritize self-care. Her work blends intuitive wisdom, practical mindset strategies, and the transformative power of gratitude.

Whether she's leading her children's homeschool curriculum, exploring new corners of the world with her family, or guiding women to manifest their best lives, Jennifer radiates positivity, possibility, and unwavering belief in the potential of every woman she works with. Her ultimate mission is to empower women to step into their most authentic selves, release the fears and doubts that have held them back, and embrace the limitless opportunities that life has to offer—no matter their age or stage of life.

Through her transformation journey, Jennifer shows that it is never too late to rewrite your story, step into your power, and create the life you've always envisioned.

> If you knew the Universe had your back, you wouldn't be stressing about the timeline.

@KARYNMEDEIROS

CHAPTER 15

THE POWER WITHIN: FOLLOWING THE NUDGES THROUGH EXPANSION & RESILIENCE TO FIND CONFIDENCE AND FULFILLMENT

By Jo Anne Forte

I woke up one morning and realized I wanted more. I was so sick and tired of feeling sick and tired. I would get the boys off to school, come home, sleep, or binge movies till pick-up time. I was unmotivated and uninspired; I dreaded leaving the house when I went to work with my husband at the salon. I realized I was stuck in a rut, feeling unfulfilled, and in my gut, I knew something had to change, or this would be a slippery slope into darkness. Darkness felt familiar, as it did when I battled postpartum after having my boys, and I just knew I didn't want to be there again.

My manifesting journey began years ago, but the most potent and transformational events have occurred over the last five years.

I've been in the hair industry my whole life. It's where I met my husband; I Manifested him. I outlined to a "T" what I wanted in a man. I had come out of a relationship, knew what I didn't like, and was tired of trying to find someone, so I outlined it and let it be. A few weeks later, my now husband entered my family-run business for a job interview. We celebrated our 20th wedding anniversary last summer. We've built a couple of companies, and as life ebbs and flows, we've pivoted and made changes along the way. Both of us are equally supportive of each other's dreams and ambitions.

In early 2020, I wanted more, but I wasn't fulfilled anymore by being solely in hair. I felt like all I was was a mum, a wife, a sister, and a daughter. I knew I was on Earth's side for something more profound, impactful, and meaningful. So, I went soul-searching, so to speak. I started reading many personal development and self-discovery books to help and guide me with my mindset.

I didn't know where to turn. Social media was inspiring at times but super defeating at other times. I was stuck in comparison. I saw how successful everyone was, how perfect their lives were, and how happy they were, and I wondered why I didn't feel like that. I have a fantastic husband, and my two boys are my world, but something inside me was just off. I knew I wanted more.

I had been in network marketing with a side hustle for several years on and off. I tried a couple of companies and represented different products I loved, but I slowly realized they weren't the right fit for me.

I loved having an identity outside of the hair. Being a wife and mum and working with other like-minded women was a joy; I wasn't alone. Along the way, I found incredible products and made terrific friends. I followed along with some leaders who were making waves in the industry. They were humble, inspiring, and super successful with massive organizations.

While watching a live one night on Facebook of one of these powerhouses, I discovered that a woman's event I had wanted to attend was coming to my town and that she, this very leader I admired for years prior, was travelling to Toronto to attend. The excitement I felt at that moment was indescribable; I knew it was divine timing. I had an opportunity to work on myself for three full days at this event and meet someone I was so fond of in person.

My excitement quickly turned to defeat. How was I going to travel to the event? My husband and I only have one vehicle. How were my boys going to get to and from school? I didn't want to spend the money on the event ticket, as I knew my boys' birthdays were coming up, and I could use the money elsewhere.

But something inside me nudged me to tell my husband about it.

His response was exactly what it always was: "We'll figure it all out; buy your tickets."

At that moment, I was both nervous and excited and riddled with mum guilt; how could I possibly take these 3 days all to myself? I was fearful; what if it didn't all come together like my husband said? But it always works out with what I've known to be true for years. I found the courage to trust the process, my husband, and the universe that it would eventually work itself out.

I bought my tickets. Yikes!.

A couple of days later, my husband said he had rearranged his work schedule at the salon to accommodate school drop-off and pick-up. He also contacted one of his clients, an Uber driver, to arrange a car service for me to get downtown Toronto for all three days. He said he had just gotten a few extra jobs lined up, so it would cover the cost of my ticket, which I had just purchased.

Wow! The universe is truly remarkable. I remember sitting at that moment, filled with Gratitude—so much so that I could cry.

The following week was the event; let me tell you, it was life-changing.

I remember the first day getting ready. The boys were still asleep, my husband was up to see me off, and my driver texted me from my driveway. I felt giddy; I knew it would be powerful, and I had faith it would be precisely what I needed. Yet, the drive to Toronto left me feeling both nervous and excited.

Walking through the event's doors, finding my seats, and settling in with a pen and notebook, all alone in this sold-out event, entirely out of my comfort zone. I was ready, prepared for my shift, and ready for more, and it started right there.

From the variety of speakers that took the stage, to the work and tasks we did, to finally meeting someone I admired for so long, a mentor, if you will. Aside from having my boys and marrying my husband, it was one of the best times of my life. I left every day filled with a view of life I never anticipated. At the end of the 3rd day, I left knowing and feeling I was different; I was ready to take myself to the next level. I went with a renewed sense of purpose; I had goals for the first time in ages, could visualize my future, and was content staying in my lane and not comparing myself to others. I had found Joy again, and my cup was so full.

Little did I know that the world would shut down less than a week later due to a pandemic. Many countries went on lockdown, and my husband and I were forced to close our business because we were deemed non-essential. Here we were, filled with confusion, uncertainty, and fear for what was to come.

Talk about having the rug ripped out from under you.

After wallowing in fear for a few days without answers, my husband and I had the 'what do we do now' conversation. He confidently told me it was time to turn my side hustle into a full-time business.

As scared as I was, I hopped on my laptop, logged into my product account, ordered more products, and hit the 'become a promoter' account fee. Sitting at my desk, I was staring at my laptop screen to a welcome message from just joining a new company. The leader I had met the week prior was now my upline, and I was filled with excitement. I had been using the products for years on and off and loved them, so they fit me. Besides, many others would do so if I needed it after the pandemic hit.

It was time to hit the ground running; I poured every ounce into my business. Every training, every virtual event, every morning power hour I was attending. I was a sponge and wanted all the knowledge and education I could have. I was learning how to build my business on social media and have conversations with clients about the product benefits; I was learning the impact these products and overall wellness and well-being directly have on your life, and the big plus is I was having fun. I was helping mainly women change their lives; they were having results, feeling better about themselves, getting their energy and spark back. However, the team culture was the most significant part and one of my favourites. I was a part of something bigger than myself, inspired and motivated, and surrounded by like-minded individuals striving for 1% better. It was like nothing I had ever experienced online; it reminded me a lot of how things were when we had our big salon and spa.

My husband was home full-time for the first time. We were remote-schooling our boys, and this business was helping us pay our bills. My husband, who is always super supportive, also used the products. He would use them to fuel his now-at-home workouts since gyms were closed and promote them on his social media. We were doing lives on social media together and having so much fun.

Amid the world's chaos, we found the silver lining and were living it up.

When things became hectic or stressful, and the ups and downs of the closures were getting to us, we would retreat. We would disconnect from social media, stop watching for updates on the news, and find ourselves connecting with our boys in different ways. When we felt we needed something quiet or relaxing, we would walk in nature. I discovered how much more I loved meditation and introduced it to him. I also began to use my Crystals, Oracle cards, and Essential oils daily, not just for myself but for my family. They were a saving grace to bring us a sense of calm and peace in moments of uncertainty and elevated stress.

For the first time in a long time, I was consistently optimistic. I filled my mind with positive thoughts, gratitude, journaling, and affirmations. I filled my body with nourishing, healthy, clean, home-cooked meals. I moved my body through walks in nature, on the treadmill, or with my husband for an at-home workout. Meditation, Crystals, Cards, and Essential oils filled my spirit with healing energy. I felt fantastic.

A year and a half into the pandemic and three lockdowns later, my husband and I decided to close down the family's barbershop portion of our business for good. We were operating our salon studio behind our barbershop, so when we decided to close the barbershop, we reinvented the space by opening an artisan boutique. We curated many amazing artists and displayed their products in-house, everything from macrame, bath, and body products to home decor and stationery; it was my pride and joy. We were open to the public but also catering to our clientele, which had become our family over the years, some of them supporting us in hair for over 20 years. We have been blessed to have such amazing clients.

One of our Artisans, in particular, was selling Crystals, everything from Amethyst to Quartz, Tourmaline, and Emeralds. There was also a wide array of gemstone-beaded bracelets and jewelry. All the items she infused with Reiki and the Healing of these magical little stones had me in love. I would walk by and dust a shelf or rearrange the Crystals after a sale, and the energy they produced was electric. I could feel it through my entire body. I wasn't new to Crystals or Reiki, but this was next level. There was something special, something nudging me to dive deeper. I was familiar with Reiki, as my mum had become a master 20 years prior. I remember having a Reiki session and the overwhelming sense of peace, relaxation, and overall lightness. That energy, combined with the energy from the gems, made me want more.

Clients would comment on how amazing the energy was just walking through the space, not to mention how it felt with the gems—it was truly indescribable. Even my energy was on a whole other level. There was more of a pep in my step. I woke up excited to work in the boutique. Clients noticed a difference in me, and I was HAPPY.

As time passed, the pull to dive deeper was so strong that I couldn't resist it. I began researching Reiki, Crystal Healing, and all the other amazing modalities in the spiritual world. I wanted to know about them all. I knew they were powerful, and I felt pulled to share them more and more.

And I know what you're thinking, seriously: Reiki? Crystals? That's witchcraft, black magic; you'll pick up bad vibes from someone doing Reiki, you can do Reiki on yourself, or maybe you've heard that Crystals are just rocks and carry no energy, or the best one I've heard to date that it's just the placebo effect and its someone convincing themselves this stuff works. Who knows what else you've heard about these modalities? And that couldn't be further from the truth; let me tell you some fantastic things about both: take what resonates, leave what doesn't.

First Reiki;

Reiki is a healing modality that was rediscovered in the early nineteenth century. It means Universal Life Force Energy, which is unconditional Love. Practitioners must be attuned to channel this energy through their hands onto their recipients. Practitioners don't use their energy; they are merely vessels to channel it. The purpose of Reiki is to Balance the Mind, Body, and Soul. This Energy enhances Physical, Mental, Emotional, and Spiritual levels.

Some benefits of Reiki are as follows (but not limited to)

Enhances Spiritual Connection, Relaxation, Natural Healing, Emotional Balance, Clarity, Self-Awareness, Balance & Align Chakras, Cleanses Auric Field, Balances Energy, Relieves Stress, Increases Energy, Eases Pain, Discomfort and Muscle Tension, Moves Stagnant Energy, And so much more.....

Reiki is for Anyone, and Everyone is open to receiving this kind of Energy and Healing. Adults, Teens, Children, and Pets can benefit from Reiki.

As for Crystals,

Crystals have been used for centuries by people worldwide for their healing properties. Everything from Grounding and Protection to Love and Happiness to Abundance, Manifestation, and Good Fortune. When they hear of crystals and gemstones, most people think of precious gemstones like diamonds, rubies, emeralds, and s Sapphires. Crystals are minerals formed from the Earth and come in various types, shapes, sizes, colours, and properties. Like all living and nonliving things, they carry Energy, Frequency, and vibration. Like the frequency of sound, each Crystal carries unique properties that will complement its owner, such as emitting a signal that your body responds to.

You may have heard of Crystals, known as semi-precious gemstones, and some may have heard of Amethyst, Calcite, Jade, Pyrite, Tourmaline, and Quartz. They are named based on the geographical area they were found, their mineral composition, and hardness, to name a few. So why wouldn't we want to bring Crystals into your life when they carry such fantastic energy?

By then, I had become increasingly less interested in promoting my network marketing business on social media. Instead, I focused on displaying all the incredible things I had in the boutique, and I wanted to be in the boutique more and more with the Crystals and other items.

I had to have a challenging conversation with my leader. I asked her for some advice on how to balance my two businesses. She told me the best thing was that I had to choose and commit to building my business online or my brick-and-mortar boutique, but it was unfair to do both. I was infuriated; I remember feeling confused. Why wouldn't she just give me a straight answer about balancing both? Maybe because she knew I was already halfway out of network marketing and I was all in with my boutique.

Now, after my level of growth, I realize that she was my messenger from the universe, guiding me down my path. She had always seen potential in me that I never saw in myself. She believed in me and would tell me she saw me do great things, but I couldn't comprehend how she knew. God rest her soul.

That was a pivotal moment for me; again, I was stepping into a new version of myself, standing up for myself, and I had again found a sense of passion and purpose, this time so naturally and effortlessly, but it felt so good. It was more intense and joyful and felt less like work than ever. Going to work every day was exciting and new; I loved my job. I had started making beaded gemstone bracelets and using the skills I had learned years before. I began to find wholesalers that were ethically sourcing Crystals and cleansing products, and I was thinking of expanding and incorporating my line into my boutique.

A few months later, came another decision: our current lease for our unit was ending, we couldn't come to a mutual agreement with our landlord, and the plaza we were in was set to be demolished in a couple of years to build a high rise. If we didn't leave now, we would have no choice but to leave soon. Hubby and I decided to walk away; it was bittersweet. Our artisans picked up their items, we removed everything we could and said our goodbyes to our beloved space. I cried; it felt like everything was crashing down once again.

What followed was a whole lot of changes and immense growth. Hubby went into a new concept called suite rentals, where we had our own small studio space the size of a small bedroom where he worked out of doing hair, and I dove into pursuing Reiki. I found a teacher I connected with online and began learning the incredible energy healing modality that it is.

After my first attunement, I was changed; I grew softer, more positive, understanding, empathetic, and optimistic. The biggest was that I was more in tune with my Feminine Energy. I began experiencing intuitive hits again. I started seeing, hearing, and sensing spirit; a new world arose. I had no idea that so much had to change to experience something new and amazing. I finally felt aligned and truly understood what that meant. I was in the flow; things were falling into place in every aspect, and the stuff that was falling out of place, I had immense trust and faith that it was all for my highest good.

My mind was more precise, my heart was whole, and I felt blessed and grateful to be able to channel this incredible, indescribable energy. I began self-healing with Reiki, doing it on my husband and boys. After my following two attunements, I knew I wanted to share this energy with the world. I started taking clients at my husband's studio, and they loved it.

Everyone had terrific experiences with it, and my cup runneth over.

I dove into research, learning more about Crystals and how to incorporate them into my healing practice. While doing so, I also learned a ton about Chakras and how they govern and transmit the energy in our bodies through our seven major Energy centres to every cell, organ, muscle, and tendon. When Energy is stagnant, we can harness physical symptoms like fatigue, pain, discomfort, or feeling overwhelmed, but when Energy flows freely, we are fluid, aligned, and joyful. I gained a deeper understanding of how everything is Energy, Frequency, and Vibration, and suddenly, everything I read about the Law of attraction, Manifestation, and Mindset started to click and fall into place. It all made sense now.

I continued with Reiki on clients, and then in 2023, I started doing vendor shows, selling my Crystals and Jewelry at markets and other events. I infused all of my items with Reiki energy as I'm so confident in its energy. Time was flying, and we were progressing and building our brand. Hubby was still doing hair, and we moved into a more convenient space for him. I still used it for my clients, and everything felt natural and free; I trusted my intuition and allowed it to be my guiding light.

In the fall of 2023, I participated in a monthly program run by someone whom I greatly admired. We worked alongside each other in our previous company, and I always resonated with how she trained. The program consisted of daily power hours; we would meet via Zoom for an hour daily, and we outlined our business goals, built our socials, and created offers. I wanted to branch out in my wellness business and incorporate more. I made my Burn and Release, a powerful tool I used for years where you journal your limiting beliefs and blocks and then burn them to let go of what no longer serves you. Her tasks made me dig deeper and forced me to look at my ambitions and think of what I wanted out of my life, both in business and personally.

At the end of 2023, I was nudged to look into coaching while working on my vision board and journaling what I wanted to call for 2024. I did some research and looked at the different options available for courses, and the only thing I kept seeing was Health or Life coaching. Looking into each one more in-depth, I realized they didn't feel like they were the ones for me. So, I kept an open mind and was patient that something would pop up when right. After all, I wanted something that would fit with what I already speak to clients about, something more similar to Energy,

Frequency, and Vibration, which would mesh well with my wellness business. Something that I could cater to my clients and support them on their journeys. I didn't know exactly what that looked like, but I put it into the universe and knew the opportunity would eventually present itself.

Lo and behold, in January 2024, a Facebook friend of mine for nearly 10 years whom I met in one of my first network marketing businesses decided to launch her very own Manifest HER Academy—a Mindset and Manifestation Coaching program to become a certified coach.

Talk about alignment. When Karyn posted about it on social media, I knew it would be right up my alley. I messaged her, and she even told me this was my area of expertise and would be a perfect fit for me.

I took the leap of faith, stepped out of my comfort zone, and signed up. I knew that the universe would support me, and it did.

The course went by so quickly that I attended as many live training sessions as possible, completed all the homework, and participated in our group chat. Karyn even asked me to teach one module on Chakras. It was a privilege to share my expertise with the group.

I felt like I was grooving, and my energy was at the next level. Throughout the weeks, I carried through as things popped up at home and didn't dwell on them. I had a new confidence in myself and loved everything life offered.

When spring came, we completed the course and received our certificates, and I was on cloud nine. I shared on social media that I had completed the course, was certified, and announced that I would let my audience know when I was ready to take clients.

Then, shortly thereafter, imposter syndrome hit. Why would anyone listen to me? Who cares what I have to say? There are so many fantastic mindset or manifestation coaches, so why should I even bother? Some of my biggest lessons and transformations had nothing to do with financial manifestations. I was conflicted, and it took me some time to reflect, meditate, journal, and release limiting beliefs and blocks to gain clarity and snap back to reality.

It's amazing how different life situations and experiences trigger us as we age. Those experiences are ingrained in us until we're ready to release them, and we repeat situations until we do the work necessary to let go.

I knew I needed to continue doing the inner work and healing myself before I could open myself up to coaching others. And that's precisely what I did. I took a step back from doing vendor shows with my business and focused on the essential things I knew would have the most impact on me so I could show up professionally.

I let my intuition guide me through the process: several nature walks a week to keep me grounded, tree-hugging and connecting with the energy of the earth, time for meditation and silence so I could reflect, gratitude journaling, journaling and scripting goals, time to work with my Crystals and Oracle cards, brain dumping at night so I went to sleep with a clear mind, time to connect with my boys and husband, stepping out of my comfort zone, and scripting what life looks like through my eyes, allowing myself to daydream, and listening to my spirit team.

It was a massive time of growth and expansion, and after much reflection, I find myself going through a similar process every time I feel the need to level up; it's wild.

While all this was happening, the window studio space my husband and I had wanted and had on our vision board became available, so we jumped on it. It was slightly larger than the space we had, gave me more room for when I did Reiki in the studio, and we loved it for a little while, but shortly thereafter, both my husband and I agreed we needed more; we were already outgrowing it. So, back to the drawing board we went, redefining our goals and setting stronger intentions for the kind of space we wanted to operate. We were locked into a lease, but after a mutual disagreement with our landlord, we could get out of it without penalty; I manifested! All of it, the space I had my eye on, and then when it wasn't for us, manifested getting out of it.

The one lesson I learned from that experience and the manifestation that came to fruition so quickly was that I needed to be more specific. I knew the studio had certain things I was not fond of, and I should have clarified in my manifestation that the issue be resolved before it was available to us. But here we are, another lesson learned and a moment of the universe nudging me to grow my spirituality.

I felt a deep calling to expand my healing practices. I had found a new teacher who was local to me and related to someone we worked next door to. She was exactly what I needed; her areas of expertise were aligned with mine, her knowledge and reputation were widely known, and whenever I saw her online, I felt a deep inner connection that she was my teacher. She's been in the field for over 15 years and is remarkable as a Healer and Medium.

When September rolled around, I took some of her courses, Quantum Healing and Angelic Mediumship, on consecutive weekends. Both expanded my knowledge, made me more aware of the connection between my mind, body, and spirit, and reaffirmed my connections with God and the universe. They both gave me a sense of peace, joy, and fulfillment while also helping me understand my higher self and Intuition and allowing me to connect with my Spirit Team.

Every day, my confidence was building, opportunities were aligning, manifestations I had forgotten about were coming to fruition, and I was ready to launch my coaching business. I was showing up on social media and in the studio with a newfound Energy. People who have known me for years would comment on how they've noticed my growth, energy, and confidence.

One opportunity I will be forever grateful for was when Karyn approached me and asked if I would like to be one of the coaches in her monthly membership group. Of course, I said yes. It has given me the knowledge and skill to put all I've learned, not just this past year but all the years previously as an entrepreneur, to use. When she later asked if I wanted to work with her in creating a pilot project, an upgraded version of her society, I was all in. It's been such an honour to be able to strategize and support those who I have.

My childhood "What do you want to be when you grow up?" was a social worker, and in many aspects, when a client would sit in our chairs at the salon, we would be their support system, offering advice, strategy, or more often than not being a listening ear.

Coaching with my one-on-one clients and in the group has allowed me to continue that childhood dream. It's the perfect accompaniment to my Healing Practice. Coaching has allowed me to connect with clients and give them strategies, inspiration, motivation, and accountability to make the changes necessary to change the trajectory of their journeys.

In November, I finally completed my Reiki Mastery. I have been manifesting this goal for several years, and it is an honour and a privilege to be certified and known as a teacher. I can't say enough about the modality. Everyone should learn it at some point, especially mums, even if it's just level 1, so they can self-heal and heal their family members.

With so much happening in 2024, including being asked to collaborate in this book, and the year wrapping up and coming to a close, I'm excited for what's to come. I have big goals and manifestations I'm working on on the horizon for 2025 and beyond. I desire to continue building and expanding my businesses, evolving my healing practices to include women's retreats, couples retreats, group sessions, and meditations while serving those who feel drawn or connected to me. So they, too, can be their best selves and live their best life.

Reflecting on 2024 and the years prior, so many little things manifested, and I've never been one to itemize them. They included parking spaces, clients rearranging appointments when we needed time off, unexpected sums of money, winning prizes, gift cards, and more.

For me, believing in yourself is the key to mindset and manifestation. Sometimes, you need to borrow that belief from someone else, like I did. While you work on parts of yourself that need healing, whether past traumas, limiting beliefs, or blocks, it's time to release them and be open to receiving them.

Abundance comes in all forms, not just financial, so it's important to remember to be grateful for all the abundance in your life. Think of your relationships, friendships, career, family, love, community, etc. Count your blessings, and watch how the universe will show up for you.

If you resonate with my story or any information I've shared, follow me on social media at Fortewellness.ca or visit my website at www.fortewellness.ca. I'd love to connect with you.

Peace, Love, and Light.

Jo-Anne Forte

Meet The Author

As a Reiki Master, Quantum Healer, and Angelic Medium, Joanne brings over three decades of holistic healing experience to her Mindset and Manifestation Coachwork. Her journey began in her family's salon at age eight, leading to a successful 35-year career in the beauty industry, including co-owning a thriving salon and spa business with her husband for over two decades.

Joanne's approach to healing is profoundly intuitive and multifaceted. She combines her expertise as a Crystal Healer with her artistic talents, creating unique crystal healing jewelry that carries intentional energy. Her ability to sense and transform energy creates a profound healing environment for her clients, turning moments of darkness into light.

Personal experience with postpartum depression and anxiety after the birth of her two sons deepened Joanne's commitment to helping others navigate life's challenges. This authenticity and understanding infuse every aspect of her work—whether she's conducting healing sessions, coaching clients, or sharing her crystal knowledge at vendor shows.

In her latest collaboration, Joanne opens up about her healing journey, sharing insights into mindset transformation, manifestation practices, and spiritual growth. Her story illuminates the path for others seeking to enhance their wellness journey and step into their highest potential.

Clients consistently describe Joanne's presence as a sanctuary of peace and calm. Her natural gift for empowerment and her ability to create safe spaces for authentic self-expression have helped countless individuals transform their lives.

Connect with Joanne on Instagram and Facebook @fortewellness.ca or visit www.fortewellness.ca to access free resources and guided meditations and browse her curated crystal collection.

The Universe doesn't ghost you. You just forgot to match its frequency.

@KARYNMEDEIROS

CHAPTER 16

THE JOURNEY IS THE DESTINATION: A SINGLE MUM'S STORY OF PERSEVERANCE AND TRIUMPH

By Megan Burn

She said to keep your nose above water because you don't need your chin to breathe. Words of wisdom from a massage therapy professor that I would carry with me for the rest of my life. These words got me through the hard stuff and landed my name on a college diploma. I had won that battle, but there was still a war, and that war was an in-person, seven-station board exam in Toronto. Talk about some nerves. Here, I had to apply all the knowledge I had learned in real-life scenarios with actors pretending to have sprains, strains, sciatica, you name it, and examiners watching my every move. To say it was intense would be an understatement.

I'll never forget the day I received my letter in the mail—the letter that stole my breath stopped time, and said, "Congratulations, you are officially a Registered Massage Therapist."

I worked as a server then and had to move home because my roommate went off and got married. They tell you it can take a while to build your clientele in school, and I didn't know what that would look like in terms of paying my rent. I went to No Man's Land, a suburb where the last bus happened at nine-thirty at night. Talk about a damper on my social life. You'd be amazed at how quickly I got my driver's licence and a car.

I found my first career job about a month later, working at a physiotherapy clinic in the area. I was so nervous. Imposter syndrome was strong. After all, who did I think I was being a professional? Not like I had hauled ass learning every part of every bone and every muscle and where they attach and what they do, how nerves send signals, and every little thing that has to happen in perfect time for you to give a simple thumbs up. No, that wasn't me. Except it was. And I deserved that spot in that clinic. I found myself working at a few locations around the city. (Thank goodness for that car) I was learning a lot from my colleagues and slowly building my clientele. Life was good.

About a year later, life was about to get better. It was time for me to leave the nest again. I searched far and wide for the perfect affordable apartment, and I found it. It was more than I ever dreamed of. I knew I would regret it forever if I didn't pounce on it. This apartment was one bedroom with a south-facing balcony. It was on the twenty-fourth floor, which was the penthouse floor. I even needed a key for the elevator! There was a pool and a tuck shop, and I even managed to grab an underground parking spot. This was my home. This was going to be my home until I could buy a house. I was laying roots in her and couldn't have been happier. Or so I thought.

Not long after moving in, a friend from college mentioned to me that his buddy's wife was opening a massage studio, and he thought I'd get along well with them. I inquired and met with them. She had a two-month-old baby on her hip, and the shop was still under construction. She had two treatment rooms and had designated a nice big space in the back for yoga. I had never tried yoga. They were both so kind and welcoming. I immediately saw their vision and knew I wanted to participate. I was hired. Everything was coming up, Megan. I had my apartment, a new job to look forward to, and even a good man. Things were just peachy.

I tried my first-ever yoga class. It was hard, and I remember Boss Lady telling me I had no shoulder movement. Well, some things never change. I loved working there. We used to have points on Fridays after a good week; every week is good when you open up. We'd celebrate every win because no matter how small they were, they were huge to a new business owner, and I got to be part of it. As time passed, more yoga classes with more teachers were added to the schedule, running workshops became a thing, and soon enough, everyone in the area knew who she was. Five-dollar yoga Fridays with donations to the food bank, food drives over the holidays, and many other communities outreach events came out of that small, community-oriented studio. I was so inspired. Not only to be part of it all but also because I knew I wanted to build something like that one day. But I liked my social life too. And with all sorts of friends in the restaurant industry, that's where I spent a lot of my free time—sitting at bars with friends. It was only a matter of time before one more late night would turn into one more late morning and no more fantastic job.

I was crushed in a vortex of self-loathing. Maybe I wasn't worthy of this title after all. I needed a job, and I needed it fast. I returned to my roots as a server and bartender at a little hole-in-the-wall pub, and soon after, I landed a full-time job in customer service at a local gym. I spent my days working, washing towels and putting on the face for the world, and my nights working at the pub, still putting on the face but with a bit of help from my friend Jack Daniels. There was a lot of turmoil going on in my life. Not only was I trying to figure out who and what I was supposed to be, but I broke it off with the man; my Grandpa was dying of cancer, and there was this one personal trainer who looked at me like I was not even worth the gum on her shoe. I was spiraling, and not in a good way. I finally asked that trainer what she had against me. She told me she had no respect for me because I was a registered massage therapist, and here I was washing everyone's dirty ball sweat towels for minimum wage. And that, my friends, was my last shift at that gym. I didn't leave in the best way, but I needed to get out, so I did.

Back to the pub. Grandpa passed away. I was drinking every night and still spiraling. One night, this magical group of wonderful people came into the pub. They were all volunteers for a haunted house for charity. We had so much fun that night chatting, blasting music, dancing, and drinking. I wanted to play in the haunted house, especially if it meant hanging out with this crazy, fun group.

They saved my life: the experience, the people, the fun. If I hadn't been at the haunt with them, I would have been working at the pub for their after-party. It pulled me right out of that dark spiral I was in. The organizer even offered me a full-time job. How could I say no? I worked full time, moonlighting at the pub part-time but somehow making less money than I was when it was just the pub. I remember calling Boss Lady, someone I still admired, and asking her how she did it. How was I supposed to make my life work? I felt so defeated. All she said was to come back. I almost peed my pants. Was she kidding? What the hell? Was this happening? So I did. I got to return to my dream job, and nothing would mess it up this time until something did. Well, kind of.

Six months later, I found out I was pregnant. This was more of a "oh shit" than a "hooray" type pregnancy. I met a cute boy, and we hung out for a few weeks, but his insecurities came out, so

I had bail. This was a never-before-seen time when my dad drank a beer so fast, slapping my parents' faces with the fact that I was sexually active. This was a fuck you, Jack Daniels, pregnant. This was also an I'm terrified and what do I do, pregnant. This was an I'm twenty-eight and probably couldn't emotionally handle doing anything but keep this baby pregnant. This was a hold onto your knickers; you're about to be a single mum pregnant. I'm going to have to leave my beautiful forever apartment and move home again because I'm self-employed and don't have paid time off while pregnant. So I ditched the dude but kept his baby and moved home. We tried for our happily ever after, to the death. It just wasn't in the cards for us. We were an excellent team for a while, though, and I chose to hang onto that.

I worked right up until a week before I gave birth. She was perfect. I couldn't believe I could love something or someone so much. It was incredibly overwhelming. I also couldn't believe I was now responsible for keeping this tiny human alive. Who's idea was this?

I saved enough money to have three months off with her. That's a decent time in the self-employment world. I couldn't return to the dream team because there wasn't enough open space to work with my schedule. Given my circumstances, I found what I thought would be the best job ever. I would work with a clinic specializing in pre and postnatal care. It was such a beautiful space, and it felt warm and welcoming. I loved being there. Unfortunately, my time there would end up being relatively brief. Turns out it wasn't the perfect place after all. I picked my socks up and found a job on the other side of the world from where I lived. It was forty-five minutes away, but it could take forever in traffic and the snow! This was a great clinic! It had terrific people that came with it and lovely clients to follow. I will continue to work here for a year and a half.

At some point along the way, it became difficult to sustain my financial needs solely through massage therapy. Before mum's life, I would moonlight as a bartender or server to make ends meet, but how do you do that with a baby? I decided I would go back to school for nursing. Shift work would be challenging, but there was much earning potential, and I could work around my parenting schedule. As my daughter turned two years old, I began my nursing journey. It was not an easy one, that's for sure. I'm still not quite sure how I made it happen. One neat thing I remember is that while other students came home to study or go to work, I got to play on the days I didn't work. I could come home and take my girl to the park or go on an adventure somewhere. It was pretty great. Amidst all this, I sadly discovered that my dream job, Boss Lady, had suddenly passed away. What a hit that was! The community was in mourning. I gratefully had the privilege of working there again when I saw an ad they were hiring. Her husband invited me back right away, and when I asked why, he simply said it was because his wife loved me. Eighteen months later, the studio closed, and I found my name on another college diploma stating that I was a registered practical nurse.

I worked full-time as a nurse for over a year while maintaining my massage practice during the evenings when the little one was with her dad. I was exhausted all the time. When she started school, it hit me that I couldn't just spend my random Tuesdays off with her anymore. Having already missed out on parts of her life due to shared parenting, I couldn't bear to miss any more than I had to. I applied to a program to become a registered nurse. My grades were good, and I had the required hours of work experience. Registered nurses have a lot more day clinic-type opportunities. This was the answer, and I was sure of it until I was denied a spot.

Remember how I said before that I wanted to build a community like that dream job? Well, that happens later. However, this is where the ball starts rolling. Within two weeks of my non-acceptance letter, a friend from the massage school mentioned her clinic was hiring and was busy. I met with the owner and found myself with more clients than ever before. As I resigned from the hospital, I found a yoga teacher training program that perfectly suited my schedule. It was serendipitous. This was happening, and I was getting there. But I just couldn't allow myself to succeed and be happy. Oh no, that couldn't happen at all. I seemed to unleash my little demons when happiness got too pleased. They often came in the form of late nights filled with booze. I made it through yoga school but not through a year at the job. It was a great job with great people, and it lit the fire under me to make some changes.

Change is hard. It didn't happen right away. There were a few here and there jobs in between. I covered a few maternity leaves for therapists in the area. I even had another chance at the great clinic with the great people, but I struggled with the balance.

But then I found a new job—not far from the previous one, so some of my clients even followed me there. I was honest with them about my history and the changes I wanted. For some reason, they gave me a chance and were unbelievably supportive. Life was good again. The balance had been restored, if only temporarily.

I met a boy. He was the first boy, out of very few anyway, who I wanted to date for longer than a few weeks since my daughter was a baby. He was the only boy I ever wanted her to meet. She was six now, so I had to be mindful and take my time. What a whirlwind romance it was. I was smitten. He was perfect for us. He was fun, kind, funny, fantastic with her, and terrific to me. Until he wasn't, until the switch flipped after five or sometimes eight drinks, I never knew what to expect or when to expect it, and he would become someone I didn't recognize. I knew I couldn't stay there like that, so the ultimatum came—beer or us. We were going to do it together and shoot for our happy ending. I figured I had some demons to kill, also. I thought I could teach my daughter a different way of life. Teach her she doesn't need a drink to go camping, to have a fire, or to have a great night out with friends. Four and a half years later, I'm still living my alcohol-free life, and he didn't make it past two months. What started as a one-year goal for me has continued beyond what I ever thought it would. I felt that if I was attracting chaos while in that mindset with the alcohol and the late nights, I wondered what I could attract outside of that life.

Choosing to go alcohol-free didn't magically make my life unforgettable, though I hoped it would. There are fundamental pieces of me that still need some work. I didn't miraculously start waking up in the morning or get good at putting my laundry away. I learned how to feel, find joy daily, and gain confidence. I wouldn't be where I am today if I had lived that life.

Back up here. I'm Still working at this fantastic clinic with these amazing people. I Love life, doing things, and ninja training with my daughter; we are happy. I've had her full-time for a few years now. Something keeps whispering to me. I get that nervous but so excited feeling in my belly. I decided to look around for a space to rent to make my dream come true. I was looking to get some ideas about costs and budgets and such. I came across a four hundred square foot space close by. The price was right; all it needed was a good coat of paint. With poor credit and no budget, I signed my first one-year commercial lease on my fortieth birthday. The risk was so minimal that I would have been a fool to pass up the opportunity.

I wouldn't open for a month as it was right in the heart of our busy season. I reluctantly gave my notice through tears and spent that month cleaning, patching holes, painting, and putting my dream together. I was proud of the beautiful space I created and couldn't wait to share it with the world. My first week in business blew me away. If you build it, they will come. And they did. And they liked it. It was a dream come true.

Sadly, this dream was about to come to an end. The building owner rented out the adjacent unit to a woman who was opening a nail salon. This woman was so driven, and she created a beautiful space. This stunning space came with not-so-beautiful aromas, as you can imagine. It was acetone on steroids punching you in the face upon entering the main foyer. I was losing clients, and the landlady chose not to help fix the problem but would allow me to leave my lease. As lovely as that may sound, this was not what I hoped for. Two months into my twelve-year dream coming true, I had to pull the plug already. I thought no one else would take me on as a tenant with poor credit and now even less of a budget. I was not going down without a fight. Two months after seeing my first client, I was looking for a new space to lease. It was more than twice the size of what I had and very affordable.

We planned to gut the space to make it mine and what I needed it to be. The building owner and his wife had just closed their yoga studio, so he knew exactly what vibe I wanted. Again, serendipity at its finest. He asked me about my budget; I said what budget? He asked me about my credit; I told him what credit. I was painfully honest about my finances, life situation, and everything that happened with space number one. His response to everything assured me guardian angels do exist. He told me I was not alone, that people struggle, that character meant more to him than credit, and that I just showed him mine. And just like that, I signed my second corporate lease. This one was for five years with some construction costs rolled in. Because of my poor credit, I was asked for a deposit for construction costs. On top of the first and last month's rent, that brought me to a whopping total of ten grand. How on God's green earth was I to come up with that kind of money in four weeks?? Simple. I couldn't. I was left with no choice but to wave my white flag. It was over. I had to admit defeat and explain to the owner that I couldn't make it happen. For some reason that I will never know, this man truly believed in me and wanted to make this deal happen. We came to a payment arrangement and drew up the paperwork. I got the keys a week later.

The place was mine. Holy shit, the place was mine!!!

This place would have two treatment rooms and a nice-sized yoga space, just like the dream started. The construction took what seemed like forever, and two weeks before opening day, I got to go in and start making it mine. The universe was working with me for all of it. I chose the wrong paint colour, and they exchanged it for me, so I was only out one gallon instead of two. I could only afford to buy half the flooring I needed on the last day of the sale, and a month later, they honoured the sale price for the other half, saving me hundreds of dollars. I thrifted, I DIY'd. My family helped with flooring, decorating, child minding, and listening to me cry. And my daughter. My daughter didn't complain an inch during the many hours I spent at the shop while she was there, too, but couldn't help with much. Not one word when I was beyond exhausted working full-time at one spot and renovating another. She was watching ALL of it, and that's cool. All this happened while I was training to grade for my black belt in a few weeks. It was wild. But I did it. Twelve years. After twelve years of dreaming, I finally did it. It's been six months, and it's still not perfect. The yoga space has only just seen its first yoga class. It's coming. Little by little, it's going to be great.

Things keep aligning for this dream to continue. Time slots fill up when I need them to, and when they don't, I trust in the universe and powers that be that it's for a reason, and I embrace the break. Thankfully and gratefully, I have attracted a beautiful community of clients who refer me to friends and family and encourage me to root for me. I count my blessings daily and am fortunate to be where I am. This business has given me a larger platform to help the community, just like Boss Lady did. Fundraiser Fridays will continue to be a thing in the yoga room, and I've just finished the first of many blanket drives for people experiencing homelessness in our cold climate. I took the long way around the scenic route while riding a turtle to get here, and I genuinely believe that had I taken any other way, things would not have turned out this way. The imposter still exists. I still don't know who I think I am. I can do this sometimes, but I'm doing it. Never let go of your dreams. It's never too late for them to come true. If you think you've missed your chance, just listen to the whispers.

Meet The Author

Megan Burn is a transformative force in the wellness community. She combines sixteen years of massage therapy mastery with the ancient wisdom of yoga to create profound healing experiences. Her holistic approach transcends traditional bodywork, offering clients a unique journey of physical, mental, and spiritual renewal.

As a decorated martial artist and proud holder of a black belt in karate, Megan recently won silver at the 2024 Canadian Open Karate Tournament. Her warrior spirit infuses her practice with precision, discipline, and a deep understanding of the body's potential for strength and grace. Her martial arts journey reinforced her belief in the connection between physical prowess and mental fortitude.

Through her innovative wellness sanctuary, The Wellness Post, Megan creates transformative experiences that go beyond typical massage therapy and yoga sessions. Here, she orchestrates a harmonious blend of therapeutic techniques that empower clients to discover their body's innate healing capabilities. Her integrated approach helps individuals recover from physical challenges and emerge more substantial and centred.

A passionate community leader, Megan develops and implements wellness initiatives that ripple through her local area, making holistic health accessible to all. Her commitment to "paying it forward" manifests in programs that foster community well-being and support those on their wellness journeys. Her experiences navigating life's challenges have deepened her empathy and strengthened her resolve to guide others toward optimality. Follow Megan's inspiring journey on Instagram @thewellnesspost406 for wellness insights and community updates. She shares practical tips and wisdom for cultivating a balanced, vibrant life.

> Stop playing small. The Universe can't deliver big blessings when you're hiding in the corner.

@KARYNMEDEIROS

CHAPTER 17

GRATITUDE IN THE STORM: THE KEY TO UNLOCKING MIRACLES

By Rosanne Lanzarotta

A Life Transformed: From Comfort to Courage

Have you ever felt like you had everything you could ever want, a loving family, a fulfilling job, and health, but still sensed something was missing? That was me. I had a beautiful, healthy family, a caring and loving husband, and a well-paying corporate job, but something wasn't right inside. I felt blessed, yet incomplete. I am a mum to twin girls, a bonus mum to two girls, and a bonus grandmother to a beautiful, sweet boy. There had to be more to my life, but I couldn't grasp it.

I brushed those feelings aside, convincing myself I was lucky to have what I had. I continued doing my job well and caring for my family. But a whisper inside me grew louder as life progressed: there's more to life than this. I would share these feelings with my husband and colleagues, saying, "I want to help others and have a fulfilling job." Still, I didn't act. After all, everything seemed fine—until it wasn't.

The Moment the World Changed

Then, in 2020, the pandemic arrived, bringing the world to a standstill. I transitioned to working from home, and for the first time, I had an opportunity to step back, reflect, and question what was truly important to me. Still, it wasn't the time for drastic changes—not yet. But during this time, I joined an online health and wellness group, and my journey into a new way of thinking began. I lost 30 pounds, gained a deeper understanding of nourishing my body, and found solace in a community with the same commitment to better living and a healthy lifestyle. This, for me, was transformative in many ways.

In January of 2022, the health and wellness group I participated in had a speaker on Zoom and her name is Karyn Medeiros, Certified Manifestation Coach. She spoke about the power of gratitude and manifestation, and her words struck a chord deep within me. I felt it—the spark of something bigger calling me to grow, to reach beyond the comfort I'd known. Inspired, I bought a gratitude journal and began journaling every day. I wrote about the blessings in my life and my gratitude for them: my family, health, and a well-paying job. But I also started writing down my deepest desires: a new career that would allow me to help others, the courage to make bold decisions, and the financial abundance that would ease my worries.

I didn't know how or when these desires would manifest, but I wrote them down anyway. I believed. And I prayed. Maybe this was the change I was meant for.

A Wake-Up Call

Then came the moment that would change everything.

In the summer of 2023, my husband Peter began experiencing debilitating chronic back pain. It worsened over time, and on September 16th, 2023, the pain became unbearable. We rushed him to the hospital, and after 16 agonizing hours, we received the most devastating news. The doctor, looking at his computer screen instead of us, bluntly announced, "You have cancer."

Our world shattered. I couldn't breathe. I couldn't process it. How could this be happening? My husband, who had always been strong and happy and everyone's role model for his positivity, was now facing the unimaginable. We were left with so many questions and an overwhelming sense of fear. At this point, Peter's pain worsened. Peter was bound by his lazy boy chair, unable to walk without excruciating pain, and needed a walker to take him to and from the washroom. We had a hospital bed set up on the ground floor of our home. I was now faced with the role of a full-time caregiver while working at my corporate job. I knew I had to be strong, push through this, and do whatever I could to help him heal. Again, this was not the time to make a career change with my husband on sick leave.

Before this diagnosis, Peter had been dealing with immense stress at work and not living a healthy lifestyle like I was. He had been a smoker for over 40 years, and despite my pleas, he found it hard to quit. I wrote in my gratitude journal time and again, asking for his health, for him to quit smoking, and for him to make better choices for his life. But the cancer diagnosis? It was a harsh wake-up call, a sign that it was time for change, but at what cost? While he kept questioning why me, I was thinking, why not you? Perhaps God had a bigger plan for his life and in this difficulty. I held on to a few powerful verses in the Bible, Romans 8:28 (NIV): "And we know that in all things God works for the good of those who love him, who have been called according to his purpose." This verse got me through the most challenging moments of anguish and exhaustion. The other verse I read over and over again was Jeremiah 29:11 (NIV): "For I know the plans I have for you, declares the Lord, plans to prosper you and not to harm you, plans to give you hope and a future." I continued to be thankful no matter what and prayed these verses day and night. I knew in my heart and soul that God was carrying us and listening to my prayers; I felt a sense of peace I could not explain, but I knew I had it. I felt in my soul all was going to be well. I didn't know when or how, but I knew I had to trust and surrender. All I could do was keep praying, believing, and hoping the storm would pass.

The Power of Faith and Manifestation

After the diagnosis, we were thrust into a whirlwind of tests and treatments. Peter was diagnosed with a rare form of cancer called Osteosarcoma on his right hip, and he began radiation in an attempt to shrink the tumor. But the results were devastating. In January 2024, we were told that the cancer grew instead of shrinking, and doctors recommended amputation of his entire leg from the hip down to save his life. We were told that without the surgery, Peter would likely only have a year and a half left to live, but also, if we did do the surgery, there was a 50% chance of the cancer reoccurring.

It was a nightmare we couldn't wake up from. But I realized something crucial at that moment—I could no longer sit idly by. I had to be his strength. I had to help him change because time was running out.

We immediately transformed Peter's diet, eliminating sugars, processed foods, and chemicals. I applied everything I had learned through my wellness journey, researching holistic approaches and natural remedies. During this time, Peter's eldest daughter, who had recently become a certified herbalist, crafted tinctures for his healing, and we saw promising improvements. I believe the universe was preparing me for this very moment.

A Life-Altering Shift

Then came a moment of divine timing. In September 2022, I listened to a podcast about cannabis and its healing properties, particularly for cancer. At the time, it seemed irrelevant, but in January 2024, when we faced another grim prognosis, I reached out to the man from that podcast, Lee Whitely, founder of Lee Helps Oil.

Within hours, Lee met with us and offered the Full-Spectrum Oil he claimed could help. Peter was skeptical, but I believed. We started the protocol immediately, and within 24 hours, Peter felt better. He slept for seven hours straight, and his pain became more manageable. His appetite improved, and his colour returned. The walker was no longer necessary.

A Miracle Unfolding

By March 2024, a CT scan revealed that Peter's tumor had shrunk by 7 centimeters. The doctors were astounded. They told us it was impossible for cancer like his to shrink, but it was happening before their eyes. Peter was defying the odds. By June and September, the tumor continued to shrink. By November, we travelled to another country for an injection of the Full Spectrum

Oil directly into the tumor. The doctors there predicted that the cancer would be gone within three months.

Healing and Service

As we navigated this difficult journey, I witnessed something else extraordinary: the power of Reiki healing. A Reiki Grand Master entered our lives, offering Peter relief from pain and anxiety, and I felt a profound calling to learn more. I became a Reiki Master while caring for Peter, and as I helped him, I also began offering Reiki healing to others. My desire to help and serve others had finally manifested into something tangible.

In September 2024, I resigned from my corporate job after 30 years, choosing a life of service and healing others. Peter had quit smoking, embraced a healthier lifestyle, and was continuing to heal. Together, we had transformed our lives—not through sheer willpower but faith, gratitude, and the unwavering belief in miracles. Grief and Gratitude can co-exist. While weathering this storm, I continued to journal in my gratitude journal daily for all the things I was grateful for, even though it felt like I had no more strength or felt defeated.

A Final Reflection

Looking back, I am in awe of the journey. The obstacles were immense, yet they led us to a place of incredible growth, healing, and fulfillment. I can honestly say I never imagined that my life would take this turn, but now, I know that every moment, every struggle, every prayer, every manifestation was divinely guided.

Life isn't always fair, and there were countless nights when I found myself asking, Why does my husband have to endure so much pain and suffering? It's a natural question, especially when we face things beyond our control. It's okay to acknowledge those feelings of frustration and helplessness. What I've come to understand, though, is that while we can't control everything that happens to us, we do have the power within ourselves to face whatever comes our way.

Of course at times, I wished our situation would disappear and things would change. Still, I eventually realized that I needed to accept the reality of what was happening no matter how painful it was and stop resisting it. Only then did I start to let go of the suffering from fighting against what is.? Life is a journey, and just because we face difficult chapters doesn't mean that's how the story ends.

Remember this to anyone facing dark times: There is always something to be grateful for. Even in the darkest moments, there is light. Our thoughts, actions, and words shape our lives. The universe and God are always listening, and the impossible becomes possible. When you believe, never stop hoping or believing in miracles.

My husband continues to heal his cancer holistically, and through Reiki treatments and we know the day will come when he will be cancer-free.

We can create a life beyond our wildest dreams with faith and gratitude.

This is my story. And if it's possible for me, it's for you too.

Sincerely,

Reiki Healing by Rosanne

Meet The Author

Rosanne Lanzarotta is a certified Reiki Master whose healing practice emerges from a deep foundation of faith and personal transformation. Blessed with a beautiful blended family, she shares her life with her soulmate and best friend, embracing her role as mother to twin girls, bonus mum to two daughters, and cherished grandmother to a bonus grandson.

Her approach to healing interweaves spiritual devotion with holistic wellness, creating a unique practice that nurtures body, mind, and soul. Through her Reiki sessions, Rosanne channels divine energy to facilitate healing, drawing strength from her unwavering faith and connection to God. Her continuous growth and self-discovery journey enhances her ability to guide others toward their wellness and inner peace.

Nature serves as Rosanne's sanctuary, where she finds renewal through mindful walks and prayerful contemplation. The year 2024 marked a pivotal transformation in her life, igniting a passion for exploration and travel while deepening her commitment to authentic living. This spirit of adventure and personal growth infuses her practice with fresh insights and expanded perspectives.

Rosanne's holistic approach to healing extends beyond traditional Reiki techniques, incorporating elements of faith, mindfulness, and personal development. Her gentle presence and intuitive understanding create a sacred space where clients can experience profound healing and spiritual connection. She views each healing session as an opportunity to channel divine grace, helping others find serenity and balance.

Connect with Rosanne:

Website: https://reikihealingbyrosanne.godaddysites.com

Instagram: @reikihealing_by_rosanne

Facebook: @Reikihealingbyrosanne

"

You're not
asking for too
much. You're
just not aligning
yourself to
receive it.

"

@KARYNMEDEIROS

CHAPTER 18

FAITHFUL MANIFESTATION: ALIGNING WITH GOD'S PLAN FOR AN ABUNDANT LIFE

By Tina Torres

Over the years, I've learned that manifesting is the key to creating the life you've always desired. It's not just about wishing; it's about believing, visualizing, and aligning yourself with the blessings you want to receive. But let me tell you, my journey with manifesting wasn't always smooth or easy. It was downright confusing at times, especially as a Christian woman.

I remember vividly when someone told me, "Manifesting isn't of God." Oh, that shook me to my core! As a woman who strives to live in alignment with God's will, I didn't want to do anything that wasn't rooted in Him. But as time went on, I understood something so profound: manifesting the IS of God. He wants an abundant life filled with love, joy, peace, patience, kindness, goodness, faithfulness, gentleness, and self-control. He wants to give us blessings beyond our wildest dreams. God's vision for our lives is often far more significant than anything we could ever imagine for ourselves.

Let me share a pivotal moment when my understanding of manifesting shifted. During my morning talk show episode, I met Karyn Medeiros, a manifestation coach. From the moment we met, we clicked. She started talking about her "Spark and Release Method," a technique that involves not just wanting but also releasing the doubts, fears, and limiting beliefs holding you back. While I'd heard about manifestation for years, I had never truly grasped it. I thought manifestation didn't work for me because nothing I wanted ever seemed to materialize. But as Karyn explained her method, something clicked. It wasn't just about wanting; it was about releasing the doubts, fears, and limiting beliefs holding me back.

I had a lot to release. Growing up in a family that lived paycheck to paycheck, I was never told I could dream big. My parents believed in security, not abundance. They didn't think about aspirations or goals outside of survival. Instead of feeling free to dream, I internalized the belief that life was about settling. Then, I married a narcissistic, alcoholic man who belittled me for 20 years. He told me I'd never be good enough, never be successful, never make six figures without him. Those words cut deep, and for a long time, I believed them. The weight of those beliefs was suffocating. I constantly doubted myself, my abilities, and my worth. But everything changed when I started using the Spark and Release Method. I started releasing those toxic beliefs one by one, and in doing so, I discovered the power of personal transformation.

Those years in my marriage were the darkest of my life. I felt trapped in a never-ending cycle of criticism, manipulation, and despair. I couldn't see a way out and began to lose faith in myself and my purpose. The man supposed to love and support me became the source of my deepest insecurities. Whenever I tried to shine, he reminded me I wasn't enough and failed without him. And for a while, I believed him. I lived in constant fear and disbelief, wondering if I'd ever find happiness or success. It wasn't until my divorce that I realized just how deeply his words had etched themselves into my soul.

One of the most transformative things I manifested was love. After my divorce, I spent six years working on myself. I prayed, healed, and clarified what I wanted in a partner. My standards were high, and let me tell you, I did not settle. If a man reminded me even slightly of my ex-husband, it was "block and delete." My friends joked about how quickly I moved on, but I knew what I wanted and deserved.

Then, one day, a text popped up on my phone: "Hello, friend." It was from a man I had known for 10 years. He'd check in with a friendly text every few months, but this time was different. This time, our conversation didn't end after a few messages. It turned into a phone call, Facetime, and daily chats. We discussed everything—our lives, struggles, faith, and dreams. And then he said something that changed everything: "I think we should date."

Even as our relationship blossomed, I wrestled with disbelief. Could this be my forever love? After years of being told I was unworthy, I had to fight the nagging voice that whispered,

"You don't deserve this." That voice tried to convince me that this happiness was temporary, that it would be snatched away. Yet I kept praying, believing, and releasing the fears that threatened to sabotage my blessing.

Ten months later, he got down on one knee on Christmas Eve and asked me to marry him. Of course, I said yes! That night, I cried happy tears in the bathroom. I had prayed and manifested this man, who treated me like the queen God created me to be. He buys me flowers every week just because he knows I love them. He respects me, loves me, and makes me laugh every single day. Manifesting this love was one of the greatest blessings of my life, and it filled me with a joy I had never known before.

But it wasn't just love that I manifested. Let me tell you about when I manifested $24,000 in one day. Yes, you read that right—$24,000 in ONE DAY. As a self-publishing coach, I've helped hundreds of entrepreneurs write and publish number-one bestsellers. But I didn't believe I was worth a $24,000 payday for a long time. I carried so many limiting beliefs about money. I thought debt was typical and I could only earn enough. So, I did a Spark and Release on my income, beliefs about debt, and self-worth. For six months, I prayed, visualized, and believed I could have a financial breakthrough. And then, one day, it happened—a $24,000 day. I was stunned, but more than that, I was proud. I am that I have let go of my fears and embraced God's abundance.

That $24,000 changed everything. I paid off most of my debts and started fresh. I even manifested the perfect home for my fiancé and me. We wanted to move by October 1, and on September 22, we got the call: our new home was ready, two weeks early. My fiancé comes home daily and says, "I love our little home. I love the life we've built together." Seeing how manifestation works has made him a believer, too. He's watched me manifest clients, money, and opportunities out of thin air, and he's constantly amazed.

Now, I know some of you might wonder, "Is manifesting really for me? Can I be a Christian and manifest?" The answer is YES. Manifesting isn't about replacing God; it's about partnering with Him. It's about aligning your thoughts, words, and actions with His will for your life. When you manifest, you're essentially training your brain to recognize and pursue the blessings God already has in store for you.

There were moments when I felt like giving up. When I was sitting in an empty apartment after losing everything—the marriage, the house, the job—I wondered if life would ever feel complete again. I doubted God's plan and questioned whether He'd forgotten me. But those moments of despair were also the moments that brought me to my knees in prayer. I realized manifesting wasn't just about asking for things—it was about deepening my faith and trusting that God had already set the wheels for my breakthrough.

So, how can you manifest the life you want? Here's what worked for me:

1. **Get Clear on What You Want:** Be specific, write it down, and visualize it. Clarity is key whether you want a loving relationship, financial freedom, or a dream home. Don't just think about what you want—feel it. Imagine what it will be like to have it.—The more vivid your vision, the stronger your manifestation will be.
2. **Release What's Holding You Back:** Use the Spark and Release Method to let go of limiting beliefs, past hurts, and doubts. You can't receive new blessings if you still hold onto old baggage. This step takes work, but it's worth it. It meant forgiving my ex-husband and myself for the years I spent doubting my worth.
3. **Pray and Believe:** Manifesting isn't just about positive thinking. It's about faith. Pray for what you want, believe it's possible, and trust God's timing. There were so many moments when I felt like God's timing was off—when I

thought He was too late—but looking back, I see He was always right on time.

4. **Take Aligned Action:** Manifesting isn't magic. Put in the work. If you're manifesting a new job, update your resume and apply. If you're manifesting a healthier body, start eating better and exercising. Faith without works is dead. For me, aligned action meant showing up for my business daily, even when I wasn't sure it would pay off.

5. **Be Grateful:** Gratitude is the key benefit of manifestation. Thank God for the blessings you've already received and the ones that are on their way. Gratitude shifts your focus from lack to abundance and allows more blessings to flow.

Manifesting has transformed my life in ways I never thought possible. It's not always easy, and it's not always quick, but it's always worth it. Whether manifesting love, money, or a new chapter in your life, know that you are worthy of every blessing God has for you. He wants you to live an abundant life full of joy, purpose, and fulfillment.

So, what are you waiting for? Start manifesting the life you deserve. If I can do it, so can you. Remember, God's plans for you have improved more than anything you could imagine. Dream big, pray hard, and manifest boldly. You've got this!

Meet The Author

Tina Torres is the go-to powerhouse in self-publishing and book marketing, known for turning aspiring authors into bestselling success stories. As the CEO and Founder of Pink Door Marketing Agency, Tina has guided over 112 entrepreneurs through the labyrinth of writing, publishing, and promoting their books, helping them achieve #1 bestseller status. With more than 15 years of expertise, Tina's passion lies in empowering authors and coaches to share their stories with the world—and profit from them.

But Tina isn't just an expert—she's the two-time #1 bestselling author of The Gratitude Journal and Beyond Gratitude. These transformative books reflect her dedication to helping others cultivate positivity and resilience, proving that gratitude isn't just a mindset—it's a superpower. Tina's story of reinvention and perseverance after facing life's challenges head-on makes her even more relatable and inspiring.

Her accolades speak for themselves. Success Magazine has recognized Tina as a Woman of Influence by Success Magazine. Tina is a global speaker and talk show host who lights up every stage with her engaging, empowering, and humour-filled message. Whether she's speaking to entrepreneurs, coaches, or audiences worldwide, Tina's mission is clear: to help others turn their trials into triumphs and share their stories boldly.

From her Atlanta, Georgia, home, where she and her new husband enjoy their empty-nester status, Tina channels her energy into coaching clients, hosting her new podcast, Write Publish Profit, and building her dream business. Her company, Pink Door Marketing Agency, is a sanctuary for those ready to transform their book ideas into tangible, marketable, and profitable realities.

With Tina Torres by your side, you'll gain a coach and mentor and a cheerleader who knows firsthand how to rebuild, rebrand, and rise. If you're ready to make your mark, Tina is the expert who will help you write, publish, and profit—while showing the world the power of you!

CHAPTER 19

MANIFESTING A NEW ME: REDEFINING MY PURPOSE AND POWER

By Trish Craparotta

I'm a 63-year-old grandmother trying to redefine my purpose in life. First, I must complete a few things to have a starting point. Income is the power of manifestation.

I had worn so many hats in my life that I could Identify for a time but never as a whole person.

I was born into a family of Alcoholics abandoned by my mother at age five and raised by my father, who did his best with children while working in the Air Force.

We never stayed in one place for more than two years at a time, so relationships were complex. Having to make new friends with every move, I didn't ever learn how to commit to anything or anybody.

It was not until we moved to Thunder Bay after my father retired from the Airforce as that is where his parents were, and they could watch us while dad went to work. My grandfather was a very loving man and generous, but my grandmother was a carbon copy of my mother, mean and meaner when she was drunk.

We tended not to be home much while my dad was at work because our home was always chaotic.

I quickly made friends, and my best friend was Gerry Prouse. We stuck together like glue. I would often be at her house because it felt more normal than mine, and her mum was lovely.

Why don't we set up our parents and become sisters like best friends? I would have a lovely mum, and she would have a nice dad!! Yup, that's what best friends do, right?

We introduced them, and they hit it off and started spending a lot of time together. They quickly married, and then we bought a more significant new house to accommodate the blended family under one roof. Gerry and I were sisters—YAY!!

That's when I noticed a complete change in my stepmother, Susan. She was always lovely when my dad was around but mean to us all, including my grandparents, when he was not. So when we tried to tell my dad, he wouldn't believe us and said we were just jealous.

So much for the fairy tale dream of having a lovely mum, and now we had to stick together to protect ourselves from her abuse. Physical and mental, and it was terrible e, and then she quietly told us all that she married our father, not us, and was on a mission to get rid of us all.

There I was, abandoned again by a woman I thought would be my mum, and my dad quickly retreated more and did nothing to come to our rescue. He just drank more.

I quickly started planning how to get out and afford to be alone when I didn't have a job or any money.

When I decided it was too much, I quit high school, got a job as a short-order cook during the day, served at country-style donuts in the evening, and lived in motels until I could find a roommate.

Life was so hard, and honestly, from the day I was born, I do not remember any piece of my life, and I could only cope so much longer.

I finally landed a job at a printing house, the first job where I felt I could thrive. My boss, his wife, and their two kids were so lovely that they offered me a room in their home.

I took it because life with this family was better than mine. My boss and wife were heavily involved in skiing and the ski jumping industry, so I started getting involved.

I was having fun, learning about how relationships work, and figuring out life, and for once, my mind and heart were at peace.

I divorced my entire family at this point because they were sucking the life out of me and never moving on, so we did not talk to each other for several long years.

Life for me was better this way.

I worked at a pop-US casino to raise money for ski jumpers from Europe to train in Thunder Bay, where I met my ex-husband.

He was tall, good-looking, and had a job, which were qualities I was looking for. He was also from out of the area, as he was a travelling salesman.

We got pregnant with our first child recently and married before my son Jason was born.

That's when I realized my husband was an alcoholic, and here we go again. No physical abuse; it was close, that's why I left, but it was verbally abusive, and here I was again in a familiar situation that I never thought I would be in, and now, with a child, it made it even harder.

Isolation is part of an alcoholic lifestyle, so we kept moving farther and farther out into the country. I didn't mind; it was a fantastic playground for my son and me to explore. He was just born at that point, and I could have some peace while he was at work.

The verbal abuse did not stop; it only got worse, and then we moved farther away yet again, and I became trapped in an area I knew no one but had nature to explore. He was never good with money. We were always broke and had to rely on friends to help us. We went bankrupt because we were both terrible with money. I didn't know anything about saving, so I handed all my money to him, m and I honestly do not know what he did with it.

The drinking got so bad, and he was putting my life and our son's life in danger by insisting on driving while drunk. I could not fight him. He was an angry drunk.

It wasn't until one night that we were fighting again. He threw one of our son's toys at me but missed, and that was it. I had to leave NOW because he wouldn't forget the next time.

I waited until he passed out, then packed up my child and anything else I could grab. I went to my boss's house for refuge in the middle of the night.

My husband hunted, so before leaving, I had the sense that he would be the one to end his life and blame it on me, so I grabbed the clip on my way out the door.

The next day, he called me frantically and found out I was staying with my boss, his wife, and their two children.

My boss thought it would be a good idea to talk to him and make sure he understood that this was

I tried, but he was so intoxicated and he said on the phone that he had all the pictures of us and our son on the floor and a gun to his head and said If I don't come back, he's going to shoot himself. I told him it would be hard without a clip, and he said you forgot the one in the chamber. My heart sank, and I thought about how I would tell my son.

He finally called AA and got some help and was in the program and sober for the first time we had been together. He was different, and by that time I had an apartment with my son, and he started visiting more often as I wanted to have a relationship with him.

Well, one thing led to another, and he started staying over. Then we got back together, and I was pregnant with my second son.

My husband felt that a clean start would benefit us all, so we moved to Barrie, Ontario, where I reside now. We stayed with his sister and brother-in-law in Bradford until he could find work and a place for us.

He worked at a gas station and had odd jobs, but never enough to afford his place, so the only thing we could afford was to apply for subsidized housing in Barrie. I felt so much less than a person at this time as we were spiraling out of control again. He wasn't drinking, but he was most definitely an angry and mean person who took it out on me most often.

We got our subsidized home within a couple of weeks of applying. It was a brand-new house in a brand-new subdivision. It's okay. It's not an apartment in a building with other subsidized people, so this may be good for us.

Our second son, Adam, was born after we moved into the house, and life was good. Our kids made friends, like real ones, because I told my husband that we could only move from here if they sold the house.

Well, that happened, but at that time, we were in a good position to buy our own home, and we did. It happened to be just around the corner from where we were, and I was happy because I did not want my kids to experience what I did as a child and not make long-lasting friendships.

We had some good years, but slowly, we got back into a rut of just existing. My husband found odd jobs, and I finally found a job after the kids went to school that allowed me to work around their schedule.

Now that we had more money, the problems and bills were piling up, and the food bank became necessary.

I felt so low then, not appreciated, not loved, but abandoned because my husband was always working. It was his excuse to avoid being a parent, and he missed so many birthdays and our oldest son Jason's high school graduation.

We were constantly arguing, and he wrote me a devastating letter to express his feelings because he could never express himself to me and just got angry. The letter discussed how I was not a good mother, etc.

That was it for me; it was time for him to leave.

I brought in borders to help pay for the mortgage. It wasn't perfect, but I had to do what I had to do. By this time, I had been let go from my other job and had gone back to school to study hairdressing, which had always been a dream of mine. I had built my salon in the basement of the house.

Eventually, my husband was getting remarried, and he filed for divorce, which he paid for and signed the house over to me.

We eventually moved into a bigger home in a better neighbourhood and restarted our lives in a house I Could not buy.

A few years later, I remarried, and we moved in together. The children were finally on their own.

This is not the first time I have tried to define my Identity.

The first was after I got away from my family, the second after I became a mother, the third after my divorce, and the fourth after I remarried and my sons left home. Isn't it funny how life offers you opportunities to grow and change, but also how the majority of us just follow the norm without ever exploring whether there is more to life than this?

I came to a point where I was exiting my final Corporate Job and looking forward to what was next.

Little did I know I was about to embark on a journey of how to Manifest My Purpose after retirement.

But this time in my life was a chance to find out WHO THE FUCK AM I, and that started with a vision board class led by my now mentor and Manifestation Coach Karyn Medeiros

That triggered a chain of events that transformed my ordinary life into possibilities I had only dreamed of.

Learning and studying Manifestation has changed my perspective and allowed me to embrace the Future ME!

When I read her book Manifest Like a Badass, it was like reading my own story. Then I thought, hold on—this is HER who was going to help me find ME!

After reading the book, she created Manifest. HER Academy, where I was one of the first Certified Coaches to emerge from this beautiful human being's idea.

When I learned that my beliefs were instilled in me, NOT FROM ME but from other people like my parents, teachers, caregivers, etc., I COULD CHANGE THIS!

It was wild, but I jumped in and did all the work. I had so many breakthroughs that I realized I could control the outcome of my life!

HOLY SHIT, that was powerful, but I put it to the test and started with finding an exit from my corporate job I was on LTD at this point and trying to fight for my rights. I found out the ICK of all the ways that they tried to deny me and make me return to work after approving my LTD, only to find out that they would let go of everyone in the Barrie head office.

So I got my big girl pants on, did a meditation, and called on the UNIVERSE to find someone who could help me get through this red bureaucracy tape.

It turns out that my husband, a UBER driver, had a client in the car that worked at a lawyer's office that dealt with the very thing I was going through and took the girl's number, and I made the call.

After fighting with my employer and the insurance company for four years, I presented my case to the lawyer via

Zoom and instantly connected with him. Without a pause, he said we had a good case.

Fast-forward: I had my LTD approved and paid out in full, and I received the back pay from CPP and my employer within 14 days.

I was free!! THIS MANIFESTATION SHIT IS REAL, and I wanted more, e and Karyn kept creating more, and I did not hesitate to say YES to anything.

Another part of my Manifestation journey was that my old employer still controlled my pension, and I wanted it out.

I called the company that held it, and they denied me, saying it was impossible. I called my old employer, and they said the same thing because my pension was locked, and I could not move it.

I was about to resign, but I thought there was no way I could control my money, so I again asked the university for a female Financial Planner to come forward and help me with this because I did not have the experience. In these types of things, I was not 65 yet.

After one week, my bank called me to discuss my investments. I asked if anyone at the bank could help me move my

Pension. She said yes because they now have a financial planner who just joined their team and specializes in this area.

I made the appointment, and when I got there, I sat at her desk and explained everything to him. She calmly looked at me, grabbed my hand, and said, "It's okay. I can help you move your pension and unlock a portion of it so you have some income to draw from until you turn 65."

I was shocked, and I cried. She also said this would take a few days to complete, but you would only be here for 15 minutes, and I would handle the rest.

We completed the paperwork, and it was done. I left and sent her some referrals because I knew many colleagues were in the same boat.

Because I sent her the referrals, she treated me to a beautiful lunch. We got to know each other, and we are good friends today.

She completed everything in three days, and now I was completely free and in control of my finances. It was such a fantastic experience.

This experience from one person who put me on my path changed my life trajectory and purpose.

This experience profoundly impacted my life. I am now a Certified Manifestation and mindset coach, learning the secret to finding their life's purpose using the power and leverage of Manifestation.

If you ever wonder if this is all there is to life, I challenge you to reach out. Let's have a conversation because there is a manual to life called Manifestation. If I can reinvent myself at 63, then you can, too.

In the meantime, you can reach me at patriciacraparotta@gmai.m, on Facebook as Trish Craparotta, or Instagram as @trish_craparotta.

Meet The Author

Trish Craparotta is a Certified Manifestation and Mindset Coach passionate about empowering women to break through limiting beliefs and create abundant, purposeful, and joyful lives. With her signature framework, The Clear Path Method, Trish guides women through a transformative process of Release, Surrender, and Reset, helping them manifest their deepest desires while aligning with their most actual potential.

Drawing on her expertise in mindset shifts, gratitude practices, and the power of intentional living, Trish inspires her clients to overcome obstacles, release self-doubt, and step into their greatness. Her work is rooted in a deep belief that every woman has the power to attract the success, fulfillment, and joy they deserve — and it's her mission to help them realize it.

As a sought-after coach and teacher, Trish has impacted countless women, showing them how to harness the power of their thoughts, emotions, and actions to create the lives they've always dreamed of. Whether through one-on-one coaching, group programs, or speaking engagements, Trish's authentic approach and transformational strategies have helped women embrace change and confidently manifest their dreams.

Trish is also excited to announce the upcoming release of her book, a powerful guide that will share her life-changing principles and personal insights with a broader audience. She can't wait to share her journey with readers and help them embark on their path to manifestation and self-discovery. Stay tuned for more details—this book will surely be a game-changer!

CHAPTER 20

AGAINST ALL ODDS: A MANIFESTATION STORY OF STRENGTH, FAITH, AND SUCCESS.

By Valerie Taylor

Whether you think you can or can't, you're right.

I was tired, buried in debt, and starting my life over from ground zero—his time, with four kids in tow.

My name is Valerie, and this is my story...

I went from being married with four children, living abroad, and thinking I had this picture-perfect life, within a couple of weeks, becoming a single parent and moving back to Canada while on Maternity leave with only four suitcases, a stroller, and four kids.

I had no plan and no idea what I was going to do. I needed a home for my children, and I had zero savings. Being on maternity leave, I had next to no money.

I had the vision and belief that I would make this happen because, after everything we had been through, I would make it and give my children a home. I wrote it out daily, researched it, and would not stop until I made this happen. Somehow, this was going to come together.

After returning to Canada, I spent a short time in Newfoundland. Then, I knew I needed to go home with my family and figure out my life. My car and the divided contents of my European home came over via sea container, so we packed up and drove home to Ontario.

I landed a job shortly after and started immediately trying to find something I could afford. I got denied by the bank to buy a house because I was not at my job long enough. They wanted to see me there for 6 months minimum.

We were living with my parents, and while I appreciated their help with all of my heart, we needed our own space, our new start, and a place to call home.

I should start looking for somewhere to rent. I landed upon the perfect house, where everyone had their bedroom and a fenced-in yard. The kids didn't need to change schools; they had already had so much change. I needed them to be some sort of regular and constant in their lives. I so badly wanted to buy a house; that was my dream, and I didn't give up on that dream. I knew this was just a hiccup along the way.

About two months after we moved into the rental, I received a call from the real estate agent I had been working with previously. He found the perfect house and had an offer to make me. That sounds confusing. I wanted to hear about this, so I met him for coffee. His wife offered me a rent-to-own type of contract as an investment for her. They would buy the house, and he would immediately write an offer with a year closing date. A portion of my rent would go to the down payment each month, which I would use as my down payment along with what I could take from my retirement plan. I was excited and scared all at the same time. I needed to see the house to make sure it was something I could take on, and then there was the issue: I just locked into a 1-year lease.

Let me tell you, a normal person would not have walked but would have run from this house. Envision for a minute. Wall-to-wall shag carpet. Falling wallpaper, a dated kitchen, and a closed-in front porch that needed some profound love. Was this something I could even take on?

I went home oddly excited. I knew this was it—this would be where my children and I would start over.

The real estate deal included the cost of the renovations needed to improve the cosmetics (e.g., removing the wall-to-wall carpets and replacing drywall where required). The house had good bones, and the wiring had been updated. However, the cost of the renovations put me at the top of my budget for buying, and it meant I would need to put in some elbow grease to make it a home.

I explained my situation to my landlord, who let me out of my lease for free.

We moved in two months later. I painted the entire house— A two-story, four-bedroom Victorian home with a basement. I slowly changed out the fixtures and added a dishwasher.

The next hurdle was having the house appraised. I needed to be approved for a mortgage that covered renovations, and the appraisal was required to allow that. One year later, the bank officially accepted my application for a mortgage, and I officially owned my own home.

This is the power of manifestation. You can shape your reality by aligning your thoughts, emotions, and actions with your desires.

Insert eye roll. Trust me, I've heard it all, but the truth is that I have received everything I have today through manifestation. The energy put into the universe allows me to receive it back.

My story doesn't end there; that was just the beginning. Becoming a single parent meant working full-time, and I missed out on so many of my children's lives. I couldn't afford to take time off, vacation days were saved for sick days with my kids, and I had to rely heavily on my Mum to help with doctors and dental appointments. I missed school awards and everything in between. I knew I needed to find a way to leave my corporate job while still earning the same or better income. I had no idea how to make that happen. Where does one even begin?

In May 2017, a friend was hosting an online party. It's a makeup company I had never heard of, but I just turned 40. As a single parent with kids all in competitive sports, the running joke was that I lived in my car because I went from my office to either a hockey rink or a barn to watch my daughter ride horses or do gymnastics. There was very little time or money left for Mama. So I decided to join this party and treat myself to some makeup. I ordered a little bundle and joined for the discount to save where possible. A short time later, I received a message asking me how I liked my new makeup, and I told her, "To be honest, I feel like a completely new woman." I thanked her and went about my business. A couple of days later, I would get another message asking me if I had ever considered doing what she does. I hadn't, but when I thought about how it made me feel to take care of myself again and how it made my confidence grow, I thought there must be other women out there who needed this as much as I did, so I took a leap of faith. I went all in!! In fact, within a year, I took a weekend course to become a certified makeup artist because I fell in love with art. I quickly moved up in the company I was with. I wanted to teach women how to grow a business and show them how to find themselves again. I wanted to help women change their lives because I was watching mine change, and it was everything I didn't know I needed.

On February 24, 2020, I retired from the corporate world. I still work full-time in my beauty business, but on my terms. Since then, I haven't missed anything in my kids' lives, which is the ultimate dream come true.

In August 2024, my daughter was set to head off to college. We had everything in place. She got into the residence and selected her roommate. She was ready to go!

She received an email the day before her move-in date with her roommate confirmation, but it wasn't who she selected, so she called to get it sorted out. The school changed her roommate, but then they said, "Wait. " To our surprise, they informed us that my daughter was not registered for a course!! We were mind-blown. How could this be? We paid the deposits and received all of the information. She was in residence and had a roommate, so how?

The school made a colossal error, and her spot was lost. The only way she would get in was if a spot opened up, and what's worse, this was the last opportunity to pursue her selected career path at this school as they were closing the program. We were devastated. I spoke with Dean, who said he wanted to be honest; the chances were slim that a spot would open.

So I told my daughter, "We gotta manifest this!" She responded, "We do." She packed a suitcase, pillow, and blanket and moved to her residence with the full intention of starting her program.

My daughter checked with admissions daily for a week, and there were no openings. It's gonna happen when I tell you how much we wrote it down and how much we said the whole time. We truly put it out into the universe.

A few days later, I sent emails saying a spot had opened!!!!

We moved her entirely into her residence on her Birthday.

I asked her if she was okay with sharing that story, and she responded,

"Ya sure, idc. I'm always manifesting my stuff".

Manifestation is about turning your thoughts, feelings, and beliefs into reality through focused intention and alignment with your desires.

Here are my best tips to start manifesting your dreams into reality.

Ask for what you want. Be crystal clear about what you want. Visualize it and write it down. The more precise you are about your goals, the more effective your manifestation process will be.

Upgrade your beliefs: Replace beliefs of scarcity and unworthiness with more positive beliefs.

Change your mindset: Mindset is central to manifestation. Focusing on what you want, not what you don't like, helps to attract the desired outcomes.

Raise your Vibration and Energy: Everything in the universe is made of energy, including your thoughts. By raising your vibration (through gratitude, meditation, etc.), you align yourself with the energy of your desires.

Take Action: Manifestation isn't just about thinking. You have to take action toward your goal. When opportunities arise, act on them with confidence.

Become a gratitude junky: Being grateful for what you already have and for everything that is on its way can speed up the process. Gratitude shifts your energy into a more abundant state.

Trust and Patience: Trust the process and the timing of the universe.

Manifestation requires patience; what is meant for you will come when it is correct.

Align with our Purpose: Manifestation works best when your desires align with your life purpose or values.

Regardless of our goal and what we try to manifest, aligning our energies is key.

You've got this, and you can truly change your life through the power of manifestation. I believe in you; the question is, are you ready to believe in yourself?

Meet The Author

Valerie Taylor is a dynamic and accomplished woman who effortlessly balances multiple roles with grace and determination. As a devoted wife, loving mother, and compassionate mentor, she exemplifies leadership and commitment in her personal and professional life. Certified as a Manifestation and Mindset Coach, Valerie uses her expertise to help individuals break free from self-limiting beliefs and negative self-talk. Through her coaching, she empowers others—especially women—to recognize their innate potential and align their mindset with their desired outcomes, enabling them to succeed on their own terms.

Beyond her coaching practice, Valerie is a successful entrepreneur. She co-owns a thriving towing company with her husband and leads a top-performing team in the Network Marketing industry in Canada. Her entrepreneurial spirit also extends to her work as a Certified Makeup Artist, showcasing her versatility and creativity across diverse fields.

Outside of her professional endeavors, Valerie is deeply passionate about DIY home renovations, landscaping, and cooking. Known for her keen eye for detail and her creative approach to everything, she brings a unique blend of artistry and practicality to everything she does. Her love for food reflects her nurturing spirit and ability to create beauty and functionality in her world.

Valerie's mission is clear: to help women overcome self-doubt and limiting beliefs by aligning their energy with their goals. She is dedicated to guiding others in using the power of mindset and manifestation to create the life they truly desire while fostering a supportive and empowering environment for growth and success.

Follow Valerie's journey: Facebook: @valerietaylor

Instagram: @valerie.t.taylor.

CHAPTER 21

FROM HOT MESS TO HEALING: HOW MY DARKEST DAYS LED TO MY GREATEST TRANSFORMATION

By Victoria Lefebre

"The gentle morning breeze flows in through the open windows; it's warm but refreshing simultaneously. It's moving the light and flowy white linen sheers in a way that looks like a beautiful dancer gliding across the stage. The movement is just enough to let the sun shine through, caressing my cheek with the warmth of the golden morning light. I blink my eyelashes in an attempt to open my eyes fully. I watch the curtains dance in the morning breeze, the white sheer linen a perfect frame for the huge window that looks out over the mountain ridge. I stretch and wake up my body, then pull the taupe, satiny, cool bamboo sheet up to my warmed cheek as I curl back under the oversized white duvet. The breeze is a welcome guest in our room this morning, inviting me to curl up and stay just a couple more minutes in our overstuffed king bed. I look up to the high vaulted pine board ceiling, brightly painted in a coastal whitewash, the considerable wood and wicker fan in the middle gently swirling. It was a glorious morning, just like all the others before it."

Taking a long sip of my delicious hot coffee, I put down the journal. My mind begins to focus on the flow of the curtains; I pause and think, "Why do I deserve such beauty?" "Who do I think I am? How is this the life I deserve?"

I wish I could say life has always been beautiful, but I can't. I spent most of my life struggling to make ends meet and find more paychecks than Months. I struggled to love myself, believe in myself, and give myself the same love and kindness I so willingly gave others. I know I am not the only one who feels these dark moments. If you are reading this, you are nodding and whispering to yourself, Gawd, me too. Have you ever felt like it just can't get any worse, and then it all comes crashing down faster than you can finish that sentence? That was about 5 years ago for me. Let me take you back to a time when I was in probably the darkest spot I have ever experienced in my life. I want to take you back and walk you through this because if you are where I was, you need to know that it gets better; yes, you fucking can, and you just can't give up entirely on yourself.

In these moments, I felt like EVERYTHING had fallen apart, including my marriage. That was hanging by a thread. It felt like the person I had once loved so deeply had become a stranger. We were no longer partners; we were resentment-filled roommates, coexisting in the same space but not truly seeing or hearing each other. Conversations had become rare, and when we spoke, they were often laced with bitterness and anger. His new personality had utterly taken over, and he was not the person I loved. I was so filled with rage and shame for the way that my body had suddenly changed that I was rejecting him, not just physically but emotionally and mentally. Feeling stuck in the narrative that I didn't deserve to be loved because of how different I was becoming. The dreams we had built together now felt like shattering into a million jagged pieces. It was as if the very foundation of what I had relied on for so long was crumbling beneath my feet. It's a feeling that I know so many of you can relate to. You just can't find the words to describe how broken it all feels, how precarious it is.

As if these shifts weren't enough, then came the shock of losing our jobs when the governments closed everything and deemed us unessential. We had no income; everything felt even more fragile. You know the feeling when everything you cling to for a sense of security is ripped from your grasp, and you are just there, feeling so raw and vulnerable? That was me. I remember lying awake at night, staring at the ceiling, terrified of the future. Those savings, once a cushion to soften the blow of aging, now felt like nothing more than a fleeting hope. The weight of uncertainty pressed down on me so heavily that it was hard to breathe. How would I put food on the table when I barely had enough savings to pay for the hydro?

Meanwhile, my boys, each struggling in their way, were suffering, too. The isolation that came with the pandemic and the abrupt switch to online schooling hit them like a tidal wave. They were lost, unsure how to navigate a world that no longer made sense. I could see it in their eyes—desperation, confusion, loneliness—and I couldn't fix it. I am the Mum, the fixer of everything, yet I couldn't make the world stop spinning out of control for them. Mum, I know you know this feeling all too well, the sense of being completely useless when there is nothing you can do to change all the outside circumstances.

I was trying to stay strong as " the mum, the wife, the sister, the daughter" but was crushed by the loss of my closest friend. Losing someone so near and dear to me, especially during her most agonizing battle with cancer, left a hole in my heart that still echoes today. She wasn't just a loved one; she was my absolute best confidant, my rock, the one I turned to for comfort, guidance, and laughter. When the world, in its misguided effort to keep us "safe," told us we couldn't be by her side, it felt like the rug was pulled out from under me. Being separated from her, unable to offer the touch or words she so desperately needed, was a pain that words can't fully capture. The isolation of knowing that I couldn't comfort her in those final moments—when she needed us most—was unbearable. It was as though the very essence of what it means to love and care for someone was stripped away, leaving a silence that no amount of time or distance could ever heal.

I felt like the chaos would never end and that I would NEVER find a way out of all this. As if that wasn't enough, my oldest son was involved in a terrible snowmobile accident. The phone call that came that day still haunts me. The images in my mind of him lying there, broken, helpless, filled me with a gut-wrenching panic. A significant leg fracture, a minor neck fracture, and the brutal reality of a long recovery ahead. When I heard he would need a rod and pins to repair the damage, my entire world paused, like I was frozen in time. The thought of my child enduring so much pain—physically and emotionally—was too much to bear. I felt utterly helpless, as if my heart was being ripped out of my chest. It was a constant battle between holding it together for him and shattering it into a million pieces from the weight of it all. A struggle every mum knows too well.

Get this: all this is happening while perimenopause hormonal chaos hits me like a freight train. My body seemed to betray me in every way possible. The weight gain came so suddenly and uncontrollably that I could barely recognize myself. It wasn't just about the physical changes—it was the anxiety that gripped me, squeezing tighter with each passing day, and the complete disappearance of my libido, making me feel disconnected and alone in my own body. The exhaustion was suffocating, a weight that pulled me deeper into the bed each morning. Have you ever felt that profound exhaustion in your bones that you just want to stay under the blankets and never come out? Me too. There were days when I had to force myself out of bed; my body felt made of lead, and my mind was foggy and overwhelmed. It felt like I was living in constant, overwhelming chaos with no escape.

Through every heartbreak, every loss, and every struggle, I felt as if the ground beneath me was constantly shifting and breaking away. I couldn't escape the overwhelming feelings of helplessness, fear, and isolation. It was as if the very people who should have been my support system—those who were supposed to understand and hold me up—had turned away, leaving me to face these storms alone. I couldn't decide if they had abandoned me or if I had gone so deep inside my chaotic world that I had abandoned them. It was a time when I felt lost and abandoned, as though my foundation had somehow turned on me at my lowest moment, yet I thought it was too much even to begin to let anyone in, knowing they would NEVER understand. How could they? The anger, confusion, and sorrow tangled together in a way that seemed impossible to untangle. Yet, somehow, I knew I had to keep going. I had to survive for them, me, and all of us. But in those moments, survival felt like all I could manage. If I drank enough coffee, I would make it, ya know?

I felt for years that I had completely lost who I was, who I was meant to be, and I felt like I had become a cog in the machine of life, feeling exhausted all day. (despite the insane coffee addiction I was sporting). Stressed, overwhelmed, perimenopause kicking my ass. Bloated, gaining weight so fast I didn't recognize myself, life falling apart at every seam. My 4o's becoming this decade of complete chaotic breakdown instead of the "FUCK THIS I AM FORTY" mentality I had been promised by society. Giving in to the belief that this was all there was for way too long; I was supposed to be broken and live up to other people's expectations. Never being able to see that Abundance and wealth are birthright to every human, and feeling so guilty when I started to rise out of the narrative that I was meant to stay in these struggles my whole life.

Why does that happen to us? Why do we feel guilty when we are trying to better ourselves? I grasped for connection with other women who were feeling this / or had felt this before. That is key to getting out of this chaotic shit storm, ladies, COMMUNITY! Had it not been for that business class that connected me to a Facebook post that connected me to this woman who promised that her method would bring you abundance, I would not be where I am today. And that's the truth. It took these two powerful women to see something in me that I didn't see in myself to start to pull me up. Sometimes, that's what we need: someone you barely know, someone who doesn't know all your baggage, to just see you at face value and believe you can. Their pull ignited this fire and cleared the storms to bring me to this spot.

The rooster crow brings me back to the room. I sit here with my coffee, looking out to our beautiful yard and swaying palm trees. I pick up my journal again and continue to read;

"The tic-tic-tic of the gas cooktop coming on echoes down the hall. My husband is preparing our morning coffee. He is more of a morning person than I am; he likes to get up with the sun to meditate, read, and journal, leaving me to spread out and take up the entirety of our bed and snuggle in under the cool bamboo sheet, overstuffed duvet, and gloriously fluffy cooling pillows for one more hour of deliciously satisfying sleep. I lay here most mornings in awe of this life, thanking God and all the powers of the universe for this impressive and beautiful day that I have been gifted once again. Although it is hard to get out of this heaven-on-a-cloud bed, I hear the gurgling of the stovetop coffee pot, the new one I just got that brews four cups at a time. It is beautifully enameled white and super posh, signaling my coffee is ready. I feel so elegant pouring coffee from it now; I just giggle. Who would have thought…me—POSH, ELEGANT —it's funny.

As I get out of bed, the cool tile floor reminds me that some days I still need my slippers. I slide my feet into my favourite moccasins, the ones I brought down from Canada, despite being told by many friends that I would never need them. They are worn down now, no longer fluffy, but just enough of a barrier to cushion my soul and comfort my toes. I make my way to our ensuite to start my morning routine. It is a big open space that feels like a spa experience every time I walk in. The back wall has an oversized print that says "I am Worthy," with my wall plants framing it. Under the print sits our giant floating two-person soaker tub, settled in by the windows overlooking the mountain ridges and beautiful ocean waters. To my left is the walk-in "party shower"—as the boys call it. The ocean blue glass tiles on the floor bring a pop of colour to the spa white experience. You are transported to another world when you stand under the giant rainheads and close your eyes. I walk up to the sink, the beautiful blue sessel reminding me of the sea glass we collect at the beaches. It sits atop the hand-carved vanity made just for us by a good friend. I look in the mirror, my face tan, my eyes crisp blue like the sink, my long wild hair with all its natural sun-kissed highlights covering my shoulders. "Thank you, thank you, thank you for believing in me," I say to myself in the mirror, just like every morning before, as I wash my face and massage my castor oil serum, fresh from the islands, all over my skin. It is the secret to youthful skin. I pause for a moment to take in this beautiful sanctuary filled with the golden light of the morning sun.

Walking into the shared space of our home, I take in the view from the wall of glass doors across the back of the space my husband has already opened. Our house is small, but it suits us perfectly. There are three bedrooms and two bathrooms. The other bedrooms are a fair size and welcome family and friends when they visit. The second bathroom is modest, more like a mini spa, and not as "escape-like" as our ensuite, but still calming and relaxing. Our shared space is an open concept. To my left is the L-shaped kitchen and large breakfast island. The whole kitchen is handmade by a friend who made our ensuite vanity. It is so unique and receives many compliments. The bottom cupboards are light natural white-washed wood, and the uppers are open shelves that frame the large window above the deep porcelain sink. My husband is standing at the stove, my coffee mixed and in hand, as he turns to greet me. The smell of the coffee, freshly roasted right here on the island, wafts up to greet me. I take a deep breath, enjoying the aroma of every cell in my body. I give him a gentle, sweet kiss and good morning as I take my coffee and head out to our big porch. We no longer have to rush our days; this slow pace feels right.

In the living space, I have created a little oasis. The cream-coloured corner sectional is flanked by a bunch of large potted plants, a big brass floor lamp that lights up the corner for reading after the sunset, and a cozy cotton blanket draped over the corner. I love that we have plants all over this space, including the ones hanging in the giant wall of windows in the front. I had my husband install a rod just for them. We walk out to the porch, a large screened-in area that spans the whole front of the house. I can see the lemon and lime trees from here and note the bright and ripe fruits I can pick for later today. As we enjoy our coffees and a slow start to the day, I make a mental checklist of all the tasks ahead for me. After my coffee, meditation, journaling, and movement practice, I have the honour of hopping on as a guest speaker today for a well-known podcaster. I am being interviewed to speak about my books and courses that help thousands of women create a life of balance and ease in midlife."

I sat in awe; I could not believe I just read my five-year manifestation journal entry from less than a year ago, and as of right now, it has come true—and more than 4 years ahead of schedule. I am sitting in our Caribbean house reading this entry as I prepare for my chapter, looking out my giant wall of windows, the linen curtains dancing in the breeze. The sun kisses the top of the mountain range as it prepares for the day ahead. I can smell the fresh limes on the tree in the backyard and the couch I sit on. A cream-coloured sofa, not a sectional but still pretty darn close, and my plants? They are starting to grow and thrive; this will soon be the little indoor oasis I so carefully envisioned.

I would love to tell you that this magically appeared after I wrote that I wanted a life like this in my journal over ten years ago when the vision was first gifted to me. That I could retire and move to my dream life struggle-free. Did I believe it when I was first given the vision 10 years ago? Did I believe in myself enough to know I was worthy of it? Nope, it would take me years of lessons, re-writing this story, of failing, of devastating loss, of complete and total frustration. I gave up so many times along this journey. It was ten years in the making because I lost sight of myself and who I wanted to be many years ago. I got lost in trauma, recovering from accidents, Narcissist abuse, my marriage falling apart, and perimenopause hitting me so hard that I just didn't know who I was anymore. I got so tangled up in being who others needed and wanted me to be that I completely forgot who I was, who I had wanted to be, who that crazy, fun little curly-haired blonde girl danced around pretending to be when she grew up. Fun, alive, and carefree. It wasn't until I felt like I had lost everything that I could start to rebuild my life how I had wanted all those years ago.

Like many, COVID took our jobs, life savings, and connections to loved ones. We were broke, we panicked, and we fell apart. The stress of life ripped into our marriage until we became roommates trying to pay bills. Online school was a complete disaster, and our kids struggled with keeping up, affecting their mental health, friendships, and community. I felt utterly broken, alone, and useless on so many levels.

This dream took a back seat while I felt I needed to struggle to put us back together and repair how broken things were. I felt the pressure to fight for everything and everyone, determined to put life back "to normal." and escape the chaos. I felt like I had lost myself, yet simultaneously, I realized that the me I thought I had lost was just a figment of other people's imagination. She was just who they needed her to be; she wasn't me. I wanted to fight to get myself back, but I had no idea who that was or what I was fighting for.

When I turned 40, I thought all this would change; I would finally step into my F-This Forties as so many told me I would. I would have this magic AH-HA moment to give me the clarity I sought. "AH, That's who I AM!!" Somehow, I would just know; I would wake up at 40, fabulous, and finally aligned with my dharmic path! Instead, the day came in the middle of the pandemic, and I woke up feeling no different. I woke up still lost, chaotic, and consumed by life. I didn't realize I had chosen and was exhausted from working so many long hours just trying to rebuild.
I was exhausted from being a mum to three teenage boys who were rough and tough and way more outgoing than I had ever been. I was exhausted from not being able to keep up with what was expected from me: being a good wife, a good mother, a good daughter, a good sister, and a good friend. I was so exhausted from the feeling that I was failing miserably at all aspects of this life,

from the perimenopause that was creeping its way in, and yet still trying to smile my way through it all.

I remember the moment vividly—sitting on the floor, tears streaming down my face, and a thought echoing in my mind: "I've hit rock bottom. I have nothing left." The sobs came in waves, shaking my whole body, a release I didn't even know I needed. In the emptiness that followed, a realization hit me with brutal clarity: no one was coming to save me. I had to save myself. I had to take back my life. I was the one solely responsible for ME on all levels. It was my chaos. What is the saying? My circus, my monkeys? Or something like that.

Finding some clarity and stepping into a more confident me didn't happen in an instant. The following two years were a fight—a long, hard battle with anxiety, panic attacks, and the self-doubt that haunted me daily. Perimenopause hit me like a storm, changing how I looked and, on most days, how I saw myself. I felt like I was losing not just control of my body but also my identity.

For most of that time, I resisted the idea of surrender. I fought to hold it all together, refusing to admit I was at my limit. But the harder I fought, the more exhausted I became. The truth is, surrender isn't about giving up—it's about letting go of what no longer serves you. When I finally stopped resisting and allowed myself to admit I was at rock bottom, I discovered that it wasn't the end. It was the beginning. Rock bottom, I realized, is a solid place to stand. It's a foundation to rebuild on.

Surrendering to the chaos instead of constantly fighting it forced me to confront the questions I'd been avoiding: Who am I? What do I want—not for others but for myself? In that dark, quiet place, I began to see that the life I had been fighting so hard to maintain wasn't what I truly wanted. And with that realization came another gift: gratitude.

I started to notice the small, quiet moments of beauty that had always been there but had gone unseen—the warmth of the sun on my face, a kind gesture from a friend, the steady rhythm of my breath. Gratitude became my anchor, my lifeline. It shifted my focus from what I lacked to what I had, bringing clarity. Gratitude taught me that abundance isn't something out there waiting for me—it's already within me if I choose to see it.

I bought gratitude journals and connected with women who were well-known gratitude specialists. I wanted to learn more and get the scoop on this magical wonder. This search led me to my business coach, who led me to my gratitude coach, who became my manifestation certification coach. The more I leaned into gratitude, the more I felt the courage to dream again. Imagine a version of myself that wasn't weighed down by fear or self-doubt.

She was confident, with clarity, and full of purpose. I started to ask, What would she do? How would she think? How would she show up in her life? Slowly, I began aligning my actions with that vision. I fell deeply into the double-sidedness of becoming who I imagined I could become while also finding deep love and happiness in who I was at that moment.

I could feel myself aligning with this new version of myself. The version I had kept secret way down inside. Aligning with the authentic and beautiful person I had always known was there but afraid to show the world. That alignment was a game-changer. It wasn't just about imagining a better life—it was about becoming the person who lives that life. I started making choices that reflected the future I wanted to create. I prioritize my health, set boundaries, and say no to things that don't align with my goals. Each small step built momentum, and each choice brought me closer to the person I had dreamed I would be over 10 years ago.

The final piece of this process was the hardest: letting go. I had to let go of control, timelines, and the idea that life had to unfold in a specific way. I had to trust that the universe had my back, even when I couldn't see the whole picture. I had to believe that I was worthy of the life I was working toward.

When I let go, the most amazing things began to happen. Opportunities I hadn't expected appeared. People came into my life who supported and guided me. The pieces started falling into place—not because I forced them, but because I allowed them. I gained this clarity on WHO I was supposed to be and finally felt the confidence building to step into HER. Allowing isn't passive; it's an act of faith. It's trusting that you deserve your dreams and opening yourself to receive them. Allowing means you are entirely in alignment with the deep belief that you are worthy of your biggest, most insane dreams and desires

This journey changed my life. These steps—gratitude, surrender, letting go, alignment, and allowing—helped me build the life I used to think was impossible. Today, as I sit in my dream home in the Caribbean, I feel an overwhelming sense of gratitude—not just for the life I've created but also for the lessons I've learned.

I'm on a mission to help other women do the same. These steps are potent guides for anyone wanting to transform their health, build wealth, or find true happiness. Through my programs, I've watched women rewrite their stories and step into lives they love. I've seen firsthand how these principles work—not just because I teach them but because I live them.

You don't have to settle for a life that doesn't fulfill you. You don't have to stay stuck in patterns that no longer serve you. You can create a life you don't want to escape—filled with joy, abundance, and purpose. The path isn't always easy, but I promise you, it's worth it.

If I can do it, so can you. I will help you escape the chaos, find more clarity, and walk confidently, one aligned step at a time.

If you're ready to start your journey toward a life filled with joy, abundance, and purpose, I'm here to guide you every step. To help you get started, I'm offering a complimentary Gratitude Journal download on my website. It's the perfect tool to help you shift your mindset and transform your life—just like I did.

Don't settle for less than the life you deserve. Download your free Gratitude Journal now and take the first step toward a future you can't wait to live.

Grab your journal here: www.victorialifestrategist.com

Meet The Author

Victoria is a trailblazer in holistic health and personal transformation. She is dedicated to helping midlife women reclaim their power, vitality, and purpose. As the CEO and founder of the 28-Day Strategy to Harmonized Hormones and creator of the H.E.R. Midlife Method—Heal, Empower, Reclaim—she has become a trusted guide for women navigating the unique challenges of midlife.

A certified holistic nutritionist, yoga and meditation instructor, and manifestation and mindset coach, Victoria combines science-backed strategies with soulful guidance to help women transform their lives from the inside out. Drawing on her 25 years as a massage therapist, she deeply understands the mind-body connection and how it impacts well-being. Collaborating with the global health and wellness company Arbonne, Victoria integrates their premium plant-based products into her holistic approach to support women in achieving optimal health and vitality. Their passion for sustainable, high-quality wellness solutions aligns seamlessly with her mission to empower women to thrive in mind, body, and spirit.

Victoria's journey from hitting rock bottom to building a life of abundance and purpose fuels her passion for empowering others. She openly shares her struggles with perimenopause, anxiety, and burnout to de-stigmatize the chaos of midlife and inspire women to embrace their potential.

Victoria is an accomplished author who has written two cookbooks, a gratitude journal, and the DO THE WORK Workbook, equipping women with practical tools for growth and self-discovery. Outside work, she is a mum to three grown boys, a foster dog advocate, and unapologetically loves blasting heavy metal in her car with the windows down.

Ready to transform your life and reclaim the vibrant, empowered woman you were always meant to be? The H.E.R. Midlife Method – Heal, Empower, Reclaim is your ultimate roadmap to mind, body, and spirit harmony. This isn't just another program—it's a supportive community of women like you, ready to rise together, break free from limiting beliefs, and step boldly into their next chapter.

Join me today in the H.E.R. Midlife Method and take the first step toward a life of purpose, joy, and abundance.

Let's stay connected on Instagram @victoria_lifestrategist for daily inspiration, practical tools, and empowering stories.

ACKNOWLEDGMENTS

I want to personally acknowledge everyone who played a part in bringing this book to life.

To my **co-authors** thank you! Thank you for saying yes and for sharing your stories with the world. I know some of you stepped into deep vulnerability, but that courage will give someone else hope. Your stories are powerful, inspiring, and will undoubtedly touch the lives of so many readers.

I appreciate our friendship and can't wait to watch you continue serving and impacting this world.

A huge thank you to my girl at **Meaghan Mulcair Photography** for yet another stunning book cover. (Book #3 next?) www.meaghanmulcair.ca

And to **Pink Door Marketing**—thank you for the inspiration to create this collaborative book, for guiding my co-authors through their writing journey, and for editing it all to perfection.

Your support and contributions mean everything.

Thank you to my friend Christine Whitely for all he kind words in my Forward. You have been an incredible friend and mentor over the years and here's to many more successes for us.

MANIFEST THAT SHIT

MANIFEST THAT **SHIT** SOCIETY

Manifest Your **Next-Level** Self

MY MANIFESTATION COMMUNITY

Home of my viral manifestation method called **The Spark + Surrender Method**™ and **Dream Scripts**™ that students use to manifest thousands of dollars, transform into a new abundant identity and reprogram your subconscious mind.

- ✓ Weekly Live Lessons with manifestation coaches
- ✓ On-Demand Trainings
- ✓ Live Zoom Coaching Sessions
- ✓ Private Community

JOIN US AT **WWW.MANIFESTHER.CA**

MANIFEST THAT SHIT

MANIFEST THAT SHIT

MANIFEST THAT SHIT

Printed in Great Britain
by Amazon